Preserving Our Built Past

Preserving Our Built Past

A Comprehensive Guide to Saving Old Buildings

Ruth Akright

Preserving Our Built Past
A Comprehensive Guide to Saving Old Buildings

Ruth Akright

KDP Publishing

Copyright © 2023 Ruth Akright

Cover and book design: Ron Neale

ISBN 979-8-87-019698-5
Printed and bound in the United States of America.

Table of Contents

Introduction to Preserving Our Built Past 9

What is Preservation? 11

Why Preservation? 15

Where and How to Find Projects 20

American Architectural Styles 22

Clues to Dating a House and Tracing its History 37

Inspecting an Old Building 43

Tax Credits and Tax Exemptions for Historic Preservation 49

Protecting Your Precious Piece of History

    with Historic Preservation Easements and Covenants 51

Periodic Maintenance of Historic Structures 54

Greenhabbing Your Historic Property 56

Adaptive Re-Use of Historic Structures 61

Living History Exhibits Provide Glimpses of the Past 76

Appendices 79

Basic Preservation Terminology 80

Secretary of the Interior's Standards of Rehabilitation 95

Organizations for Historic Preservation 98

Resources for Greening Your Project 102

Periodic Maintenance Plan Checklist 103

Further Reading 104

Resources for Finding Old Houses 105

The Murfree-Williams House, photo circa 1900, Murfreesboro, NC

Introduction to Preserving Our Built Past

The heritage of the past is the seed that brings forth the harvest of the future. - Inscription at the base of a statue near the entrance of the National Archives Building, Washington.

A life-long fascination with old buildings and those who created them, as well as a desire to share many years of study and working experience led to the creation of this book. After earning a degree in Interior Design, my career path took a turn toward preservation and I have never looked back. I have worked in the field of historic preservation for more than 40 years in nearly all aspects of the profession from managing historic sites for non-profits, to assisting clients in their renovations, and renovating my own projects. I have watched as the need for preservation of older properties has progressed and grown. As costs of materials have risen and availability of products to renovate older properties has become more difficult, it is even more important for us to make the effort to save and rehabilitate them into viable livable homes and businesses.

It is my personal belief that we have an obligation to pass these old places along in as good as or better condition than that in which we found them. Preservation, after all, is more about the stewardship of history than the mere ownership of property.

There are many avenues for the preservation of historic properties: restoration, rehabilitation, adaptive reuse or inclusion in a greater whole as in Williamsburg, VA. These properties present us with an opportunity to live, work in, and visit the craftsmanship and lifestyles of our past. They are the architectural assets of our history and the land-marks with which we connect. They lend us a sense of continuity. To quote Tom Mayes, author of Why Do Our Old Places Matter, "Old places connect us to our ancestors and our ancestors connect us to old places, giving us a sense of belonging and identity".

The reader will be led to a clearer understanding of why we should work toward preserving the structures of the past, whether they're simple to lavish private residences or a part of an existing commercial environment.

Drayton Hall, Charleston, South Carolina

The Garrett Hotel, Ahoskie, NC

What is Preservation?

We shape our buildings; thereafter, our buildings shape us.   Winston Churchill

What is it that draws some of us to these old buildings? That causes us to lose our hearts and perhaps a bit of our sanity when we find "the One"? (Some of us even are fortunate enough to find more than that one.) Is it the mystery of its past, a sense of romance, a familial connection, or its particular architectural style? Maybe it is the knowledge that it has survived all the trials and tribulations of a long existence. All of these emotions may play into our choices and commitment to these old places. However, there are also more logical and practical concerns for rescuing and restoring them. Throughout this book, we will explore all the aspects of our commitment to the lure of preservation.

The truly dedicated and purposeful preservation movement in this country had its beginnings in the 19th century, when groups of volunteers recognized the need for saving the places of our Founding Fathers who had played such vital roles in the establishment of our young nation. Up until that time, any preservation effort was left to families who owned and lived in the buildings.

George Washington's Mount Vernon

The earliest true restoration project was Independence Hall. It was begun in 1816 and funded by the City of Philadelphia. Mount Vernon and Monticello were saved and conserved through the efforts of groups such as The Daughters of the American Revolution. Most of these early efforts became "house museums". They still serve as learning laboratories for those with an interest in older properties. Many were furnished with period furniture, often that of the original family. Because of the high costs of constant maintenance and staffing, few of these museums were ever profitable. Those which survive today are run mostly by volunteer staffs with a paid director, and are non-profit organizations (501c3). This designation allows them many tax benefits in order to continue operation. Paid visitation to the sites also aides in the preservation. The fastest growing segment of tourism, Cultural/Heritage Tourism, is to these sites.

Other buildings were saved primarily due to their architectural importance. For example, The Octagon in Washington, DC (circa 1801), was purchased by the American Institute of Architects in 1901. Some buildings of this type were converted to museums, but often they became the headquarters of historical organizations who used them as office spaces.

 In 1935 the first Historic Sites Act was passed. It outlined programs for doing research and inventories of notable sites. This began efforts in several states to identify their own historic assets. Charleston, SC created the very first historic district. Even then, most preservation efforts were left to private organizations.

Thanks to the astute vision of Rev. W. R. R. Goodwin, Rector of Bruton Parrish Church and the Association for the Preservation of Virginia Antiquities, the restoration of the Georgian buildings in Colonial Williamsburg in Virginia was undertaken in the 1920's. He then gained the financial support of John D. Rockefeller Jr., the wealthy son of the founder of the Standard Oil monopoly. His monumental undertaking in the restoration included a view of the entire town as worthy of saving, due to the important role it played in the establishment of our new nation. ⌈Here we begin to see the emergence of the historic house within a neighborhood, and how each contributes its own personality and life to the whole. Although not all of the buildings were deemed viable for restoration, many were indeed returned to their former appearance. Those that could not be saved were replicated using old records, photos, and recollections of residents. Of the approximately 500 buildings reconstructed or restored, 88 are labelled original. Thus, recreating an 18th century village that knew the likes of Patrick Henry, Thomas Jefferson, James Monroe, James Madison, and others who formed our young country. Today, we are able to visit and come away with a full sense of how the population lived and worked in the 18th century. This is "living history" at its best, thanks to the vision of Rev. Goodwin and Rockefeller and the efforts of the Colonial Williamsburg Foundation which continues to operate the site.

Courthouse, Colonial Williamsburg, VA   *Outbuilding, Colonial Williamsburg, VA*

The establishment of the National Trust for Historic Preservation in 1949 began the involvement of a government body as the voice of historic preservation. The organization's first headquarters was in the offices of Ford's Theatre (Lincoln Museum) in downtown Washington, D.C. This legislation increased public awareness of the movement and provided vital information for those who were interested in participating. The passage of the National Preservation Act in 1966 set us on the road to true preservation of our history in this country. As you progress through the material in this book, you will see mention of the National Trust for Historic Preservation often. This organization works with the public to preserve structures, and has a property listing process which we will discuss in a separate chapter. Just know that if you are serious about preservation, they are the premier organization to provide you with information and guidelines.

You will encounter varied approaches to Preservation in your quest, be it for a home to live in, a house museum, or a unique business adaptive reuse. It is imperative that you have a working knowledge of the terms used in the field. Preservation and historic preservation are used almost interchangeably, and refer to the work that enables the participant to conserve the historic fabric and features in an old structure.

Preservation is defined by the National Trust for Historic Preservation as "a conversation with our past about our future. It provides us with opportunities to ask, "What is important in our history?" and "What parts of our past can we preserve for the future?" Through historic preservation, we look at history in different ways, ask different questions of the past, and learn new things about our history and ourselves. Historic preservation is an important way for us to transmit our understanding of the past to future generations."

Preservation is also defined as an endeavor that seeks to preserve, conserve and protect buildings, objects, landscapes or other artifacts of historical significance. It is a philosophical concept that became popular in the twentieth century, which maintains that cities- as products of centuries of development- should be obligated to protect their patrimonial legacy. This term refers specifically to the preservation of the built environment, and not to preservation of, for example, primeval forests or wilderness.

The Robert Carter House, Colonial Williamsburg,

Revolution Mill, Greensboro, NC

Why Preservation?

It is better to preserve than to repair, better to repair than to restore, better to restore than to reconstruct.   A.N. Didron, 1839 archaeologist

This book will explore the reasons we should strive toward preserving our built past-whether residential or commercial - all the old buildings that still stand and are awaiting new lives. How can they make contributions to today's communities, the economic and social benefits of restoration or rehab, and their impact on heritage and cultural tourism?

It is thought that there are three kinds of people who love old houses. The first kind are the purists, who feel they should step into the past as they open the front door. They search out the traditional craftsmen who still hand-hew beams, mill flooring from old growth woods, or do hand troweled horsehair plaster. As one owner of a house in Ohio put it, "If you are a custodian of a period house, you owe it to the house to do what is appropriate for it. You really don't own the house. It is entrusted to you." In today's age how do you remain true to the purist philosophy while still having a home that meets all of the needs of contemporary living? There are many hard decisions to be made in a purist restoration.

The second kind are the pragmatists. This group loves and understands the needs of the old house, but they also know it is better to restore an old window or door if it's possible.

However, if the historic fabric is too far gone, they seek out the most efficient and appropriate replacement element that can be found.

The third and last group are the <u>revisionists</u>, who love classic architecture but would rather have a new structure. They remain true to the classic styles and traditional details such as wood moldings, reproduction period style lighting fixtures and hardware using new materials.

The debate among old house owners as to what should be saved and how, is one that is often hotly debated and sometimes taken too far, to the detriment of the property. While the debate rolls on, many times the structure is lost or ruined beyond repair.

Why are these buildings so sought after and revered? They were hand-crafted with skills and materials that are no longer available to us. They have distinct character that only this meticulous craftsmanship can imbue. That individualism is the charm that most old house owners seek. The old growth materials were harder and stronger than what is available today. These materials have aged gracefully and well over the years.

Generally, when people think of historic preservation, they think of old houses in varying states of disrepair. While residential properties are the back bone of preservation efforts, there are a great many communities that are benefiting from preservation and revitalization of downtown areas. Formerly abandoned and dilapidated commercial buildings are being rehabilitated by new or returning business owners. As more and more people become interested in the advantages of a return to urban living these buildings are thriving again, both as living spaces and business enterprises. Restaurants, boutiques, small neighborhood grocery stores, florists, art galleries, etc. are popping up in cities and towns all over the country.

Preservation is the ultimate in recycling. It keeps irreplaceable materials out of landfills and conserves and preserves architectural details that would otherwise be lost forever. Adaptive reuse- or restoration of existing buildings - conserves our natural resources because it builds upon the original building's fabric. This is in stark contrast to the typical scenario of bulldozing, hauling debris to a landfill and constructing an entirely new building. It takes an incredible amount of energy to construct a new building. Constructing a new 50,000 square foot commercial building takes the same amount of energy as driving a car 20,000 miles a year for 730 years. It takes about 65 years for an energy efficient new building to save the amount of energy lost in demolishing an existing building.

A partial renovation is as smart as, or smarter than, a total gut job especially if the property has valuable elements that should be retained (unique plaster moldings, solid panel doors, lighting fixtures, tiles, fireplace surrounds and mantels). Try to fix without tearing down. Try not to take an "all or nothing" approach that may only destroy these precious key historic elements. Before you begin any demo, consult with an architect who is familiar with historic properties. He can guide you to the most expeditious and most favorable solution for your specific property. If you do decide to gut the house, carefully remove details such as trim to reuse or have replicated by a professional. If you don't reuse them, you can donate or sell them to someone who needs them for their project. Contact Habitat for Humanity, local salvage yards or join organizations of folks who are in the process of restoring their own homes. I belong to one on-line called the Restoration Guild. They are always happy to have a resource for those precious pieces and parts. For example: shingles can be recycled into asphalt driveways and parking lots.

Restored bathroom using original fixtures – Pritchard House, Titusville, FL

Additional advantages of preservation are these:

It promotes a better quality of life; creates jobs in construction, architectural and related services; increases property values and thereby increases tax revenue; is a vehicle for sustainable tourism focusing on history and culture, known as Cultural and Heritage Tourism; revitalizes downtown areas in small towns and is an economic force which adds total spending and increased labor earnings for all the trades involved.

Today the recognized terms for the protection of historic properties are preservation, rehabilitation, restoration and reconstruction. Each of the terms describes a specific activity and has a legal meaning. This meaning relates directly to available Federal, State and local grants, programs, tax credits and incentives for which owners of the properties may apply.

<u>Preservation</u> refers to the process of applying measures necessary to sustain the existing form, integrity and materials of the property. Any work on the property will, in this case, focus on repair of existing materials and a schedule of ongoing maintenance rather than replacement or new construction

<u>Restoration and Rehabilitation</u> - You will see these terms used over and over, and not necessarily by their strictest definitions. They are very different approaches to the preservation process. Renovation is also used, but more accurately in regard to rehabilitation. Restoration by definition, means accurately replicating the form, features and

character of the property. Rehabilitation is the process that makes it possible to create a compatible use for the property through repair, alterations and additions while preserving the parts or features that express its historical and architectural values.

Before   The Pritchard House, Titusville, VA   After

Restoration in its strictest sense is returning the property to as near its original appearance at construction as possible. This method is most often used in the creation of historic house museums where the primary objective is to educate visitors in the lifestyles and architecture of the period. This process involves replicating any missing architectural elements using materials that are as close to the originals as are available. As can be imagined, this method strictly adhered to, is very costly. This can be achieved either by using materials from dismantled properties or through salvage companies who stockpile old pieces. Authenticity is the key here. This particular method is best left to professionals and expert craftspeople. If you are planning to revitalize an older building, these meticulously restored house museums are a treasure trove of history to guide you in your own project.

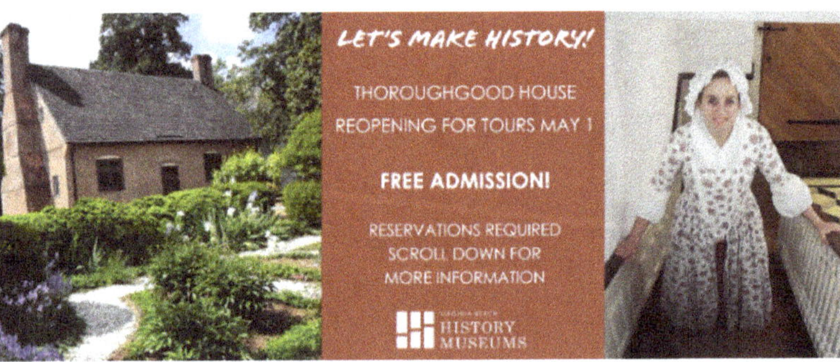

Francis Land House, Virginia Beach VA   Thoroughgood House, Virginia Beach, VA

These restored properties are owned and operated by the City of Virginia Beach, VA

Rehabilitation takes a more liberal view of preservation in that materials do not necessarily have to replicate the originals. Retain all of the old elements that you can. Because you purchased this property because you loved it and its history, it is advisable to plan ahead for your desired outcome. A finitely detailed plan must be in place and caution exercised before any demolition is begun. How sad to get to the end and find that the very irreplaceable detail that you would have wanted was the thing that got tossed away. Even here, if you can find true 2"x4"s or old materials, do it. The rewards will be greater than the cost or effort required to obtain them.

August 1985 before rehab by new owners 2020 After Extensive Rehabilitation The Murfree-Williams House, circa 1800, Murfreesboro, NC

Where and How to Find Projects

Old places have soul.   Homeowner, Sarah Anderson

Properties Available from Preservation North Carolina (presnc.org), a revolving fund.

Although it has become more difficult to find really inexpensive older buildings, there are still projects available that are affordable if you know where to look. There are numerous web sites that specialize in the sale of these properties. Look into circa.com, oldhouses.com, United Country Realty, Preservation North Carolina, The National Trust, etc. All of these organizations publish periodic listings by state to make it more accessible for those looking for a project. Each state maintains a State Historic Preservation Office from which you can gather all kinds of information that will assist you in your journey.

Some of these associations, such as Preservation North Carolina, are non-profit revolving funds. PNC is one of the oldest organizations of this kind in the country and one that has had, and continues to have, great success. They publish an online newsletter listing all the available property for renovation as well as listing renovated property for sale either by owner or realtors. Comparison of the properties will give you a sound idea of what to expect in terms of pricing differences. These trusts are often given properties, purchase them at a very low price, or inherit them from owners who wish to insure the building's future. Most are residences, but once in a while there will be a commercial structure. The trusts sell them "as is" usually and with protective covenants that require the purchaser rehab and occupy the property for a specific period of time. The covenants include items such as the necessity of requesting permission from the local governing body to choose paint colors, fencing. and other elements that can affect the appearance of the property and its appropriateness within the surrounding neighborhood. Don't be put off by these as they are for your protection as well as the protection of the property and its surroundings. The funds they receive from the sales go back into their coffers to provide monies to purchase additional properties. These will almost always require total rehabs and full replacement of mechanical systems. That is not a bad thing if you are planning to rehab and not attempt restoration. It is a great way to find a wonderful old place at a good price and give it a new life, as well as to support a worthwhile organization.

United Country Realty specializes in rural country properties including individual homes, historic homes, businesses, bed and breakfasts, farms, ranches and wooded property. They are the largest integrated organization of real estate and auction professionals. They list homes in all architectural styles across the country. Their web site is easy to use including maps of areas to assist you in finding just what you are looking for. If you'd rather, you can order their catalog in print copy. They also handle foreclosures.

A local realtor in your area of interest can be invaluable to your search. They will undoubtably be familiar with everyone in their town and know when something is going to be put on the market. Provide the Realtor of your choice with a detailed list of features you are in the market for, and your price range.

The National Trust publishes a list of available property in their periodic magazine produced for members and online. Since they charge a fee to list property, most of the houses on their list are more expensive and many have undergone recent renovations. Again, it depends on what you are looking for and how much money, time and effort you are willing to invest.

Murfreesboro, NC $524,000 2 acres   *Dallas.NC Jail $125,000 $60,000 4,000 sq. ft. on*

Examples of Property from Preservation North Carolina Revolving Fund

American Architectural Styles

Architecture is to be regarded by us with the most serious thought. We may live without her, and worship without her, but we cannot remember without her. John Ruskin

Colonial Revival, Elizabeth City, NC

European settlers came to the new colonies to make their homes, establish villages and towns, establish new lifestyles and pursue religious freedoms. They brought with them memories of the architectural styles they had been familiar with in the old country. Once they evolved past the need for very basic housing for survival, they began to form what would become a uniquely American style. Using readily available native woods such as hickory, pine, walnut and oak and making brick from the native clay, they were able to combine the elements of their remembered European styles with a practicality born of the local climate and need. In colder northern climes buildings tended to have fewer and smaller windows, lower ceilings and thicker walls to make them easier to heat. The higher heat and humidity of the South dictated more direct air circulation by using cross ventilation, higher ceilings, central halls, etc. In the Spanish territories like Florida, the buildings were reminiscent of those in Spain with plaster and tabby or coquina walls, balconies, floor length windows and more outdoor living spaces.

The evolution of these principles in particular areas became recognized styles that endured and continued to grow and change as the country became more prosperous and settled. Until approximately 1840 American styles were widely separated by region and time. That is to say, usually only one fashion prevailed at a given time in any one region.

The styles evolved from the features, materials, floor plans and appearance of each building. Primarily the placement of windows and doors, roofing material and form and the details of the architecture became the basis for the style.

As you search for your "special one", you will encounter many styles of architecture. It is advisable to become familiar with the accepted names of each of the most popular styles based on their characteristics and their history of development. You will notice as you look at older homes, that sometimes they contain elements of other styles and the names sometimes vary by region. Like anything else, as newer styles came along, the older houses were "remodeled" using these new features. It is prevalent in Queen Anne houses which often have shingles added to their exteriors to modernize them. This working knowledge of styles will be of great use to you. It will be much easier to communicate with real estate agents, architects, contractors. etc.

A. Colonial – American Colonial architecture dates back to the 1600s,   originating during the colonial period of the United States. Though the style technically encompasses English Colonial, French Colonial, Spanish Colonial, Dutch Colonial, and Georgian styles, American Colonial is most similar to English Colonial due to the prolonged length of British rule in America. As styles developed and homes became larger, regional aspects of this early period began to emerge.

1. <u>English 1620 – 1800</u>

The defining characteristics of Colonial architecture are simple, symmetrical, and rectangular, two or more stories tall with the staircase and front door centered in the house. Colonial-style homes in New England were often built with wood; those on Long Island and in the Hudson River Valley were constructed with brick and stone. Saltbox style homes and Cape Cod style homes were some of the simplest of homes constructed in the New England colonies. Cape Cods were typically constructed as 30'x40' buildings.

2. <u>Spanish 1620-1885</u>

St. Augustine, Fl

Buildings of this style were typically constructed of adobe brick, rubble stone or even co-quina shell in Florida examples. Walls were faced with stucco. They were one or two-story with low-pitched or flat roofs. Many   have covered porches running the entire length of the building which shaded the windows, and served as a passageway between rooms. Often these houses were L or U shaped surrounding a patio. This style was prominent in warmer climes such as the Southwest and in Florida.

3. <u>Dutch 1625-1840</u>

The Dutch style featured steeply pitched roofs which were covered in wood shingles or slate. Flared eaves are also a feature of this style. Exterior walls were clapboard, brick, or stone. Windows were double-hung and multi-paned. The houses are usually   rectangular in plan with rooms located off a central hall containing the stairs. This style was found in the Hudson Valley of New York and other parts of New England.

B. Tudor – 1485-1603

Tudor styling adapted by the Moravian settlers in Old Salem, Winston Salem NC

Basic characteristics of this style are reflected by their steeply pitched gable roofs, playfully elaborate masonry chimneys (often with chimney pots), embellished doorways, groupings of windows, decorative half-timbering and stucco exterior, and multi-pane leaded glass windows.

C. Georgian 1700-1830

Characterized by symmetrical elevations with axial entrances including a rectangular plan, two main stories, hipped roof, paneled   front door, wood single-hung multipaned windows with thick muntins, dentiled cornice, wood frame with clapboard siding with vertical corner boards or pilasters. In the South, construction is usually brick. In brick buildings there are belt courses and quoins. Georgian style houses   are found east of the Appalachian Mountains from Maine to Georgia. Later Georgian houses differ from early ones in the detailing. They feature elaborate cornices, fan and side lights at front doors and use Palladian, semi-circular and elliptical windows in addition to double-hung. This later style is most often found east of the Mississippi River.

D. Federal/Adam 1780-1830

The Federal/Adam style features a low-pitched gable, hipped roof. Exterior walls are clapboard or brick. Windows are double-hung with each sash containing six or eight panes of glass. You will see this referred to as six-over-six or eight-over eight windows. This was a popular style in urban areas, often becoming row houses. Look for Federal Houses east of the Appalachian Mountains from Maine to Georgia.

E. Greek Revival 1820-1860

This style relies on classic Greek architecture for its form and details. Think Antebellum Mansions of the Deep South. There are Classical entablatures, pedimented gable-end roofs, columns, and corner pilasters from the three classic styles (Doric, Ionic, Corinthian). The exterior walls are made of clapboard or brick. Interiors feature Greek key moldings and interior columns separating main living spaces from a central entry hall. It is found east of the Mississippi River, the deep South and in parts of California.

F. Gothic Revival 1830-1880

Influenced by the designs of Andrew Jackson Downing Buildings adopted a complex design that drew inspiration from symmetry and neoclassicism. Decorative vergeboards, roof finials, gothic arched windows and door heads and other Gothic details including chimneys, gables, embrasure towers, warhead windows, gargoyles, stained glass and severely sloped roofs are typical of the style. Exteriors are faced with clapboard and stucco or constructed of stone. Brick was also used and often polychromed. Oriel and bay windows are frequently used along with double hung windows. These houses are primarily found in the Northeast, with some found in other parts of the country that were founded prior to 1880.

G. Victorian Era – Houses built in this period seldom show any obvious mixtures of styles. Within this category are subcategories which evolved over the long period during which the style was popular (i.e. the years Queen Victoria reigned in England.)

1. Italianate 1840-1880

These houses were built on an asymmetrical or L-shaped plan, with corner stair towers and projecting cupolas. They have heavily bracketed cornices and exterior walls of brick or clapboard. The style was used extensively in urban areas as row houses as well as country villas. The style was popular in the Midwest, but it is also found in all areas of the country that were founded before 1880.

2. Second Empire 1855-1890

Petersburg, VA

The dominant features of the style are a Mansard roof with heavy cornices and brackets, rounded window and door hoods with brackets, and dormer windows. Exterior walls are made of brick, stone or clapboard. Interiors have patterned wallpaper, gilding and stenciling as a norm. Second Empire houses are common in the Northeast and Midwest but are also found throughout the country. The New York town of Catskill has many fine examples of this classic style.

3. Stick Style 1860-1890

The Stick Style represented the most innovative design concepts and building technologies of its time, yet it did not attract serious study or even a widely accepted name until a century later. They were almost always architect designed and were all about carpentry. They are light, irregular, and airy in appearance due to their balloon-frame using 2x4 lumber and nails. The style is made up of projecting bays, gables, porches, towers and dormers. Roof plans are complex with intersecting gables and roof effects such as clips, hoods, and kicked eaves. Look for these houses in the Midwest and San Francisco's Painted Ladies.

4. Queen Anne 1875-1900

Queen Annes in Smithfield, VA

This is probably the most recognizable and popular style within the Victorian era. It is characterized by steeply pitched irregular or cross gabled roofs, classical detailing on cornices, double-hung windows, and towers. Walls are clapboard, brick, and decorative shingles including the popuar fish scale style. The houses are whimiscal and often have multi-colors, with window and other trim being a darker or contrasting tone.These popular houses are found all over the country.

5. Shingle 1880-1890

Shingle style homes are distinguished by their exterior wood shingles mixed with clapboard stone of patterned brick. Facades are asymmetrical with welcoming verandas. Roofs are gambrel or irregularly pitched and covered in wood shingles. They are classic yet more rustic and informal than previous styles. Interior walls are often finished with wood and plaster, and ceilings are plaster with wood beams. This style is found all over the country.

H. Richardsonian/Romanesque 1880-1900

The style is named after the architect Henry Hobson Richardson (1838–   1886). It incorporates 11th and 12th century southern French, Spanish, and Italian Romanesque characteristics. Richardson first used elements of the style in his Richardson Olmsted Complex in Buffalo, New York, designed in 1870. Multiple architects followed in this style in the late 1800s; Richardsonian Romanesque later influenced modern styles of architecture as well. This robust style, used for large commercial and institutional buildings as well as residences, exhibits a massive quality, harmonious proportions, thick stone walls, round arches, sturdy piers, thick heavy pillars,barrel vaults, small windows, large towers, and symmetrical plans.

I. Colonial Revival 1890-1940

This style is derived from those styles popular during the American colonial period, particularly the Georgian and Late Georgian. It uses the same plan, elevations and details and as such is difficult to identify from the original. The major difference is the manufacture of the materials is no longer hand-made, but now precisely replicated by machine. Gone are the imperfections that occur with the hand-made older examples.

J Tudor Revival 1890-1940

Wilson, NC   *Elizabeth City, NC*

This style is typified by its wood half-timbered and stucco walls, front facing gables, front facing chimney, "skintled" brickwork (irregular bricks sticking out from wall in imitation of medieval brickwork) and multipaned leaded glass casement windows. Interiors feature wood wall paneling and wood box beams on ceilings.

K. Arts and Crafts Styles -The Arts and Crafts style had its beginnings in the mid- nineteenth century England as a throwback to a time when hand craftmanship was prevalent, before machinery began to take on a more important and prominent role in architecture, as well as all of life of the period. It was more an intellectual approach drawing on many styles. It remains one of the most confusing and hard to nail down styles of architecture, blending styles and motifs. The Industrial Revolution was a celebration of the wonders of manmade materials and the possibilities of what machines could offer the populace. Craftsman architecture was an aesthetic reaffirmation of the beauty of natural materials and forms, and the marvels of what humans can make with their own hands.

William Morris is thought to be the "father of" the Arts and Crafts movement. He advocated "Have nothing in your houses that you do not know to be useful or believe to be beautiful." He felt that well-designed, handcrafted objects were admirable while factory goods were an abomination.

In the United States, the Arts and Crafts movement also began to influence house design beginning around 1897. Architects like Greene and Greene, Bernard Maybeck, Julia Morgan, and Frank Lloyd Wright were all influenced by the simplicity and hand crafting of the designs and put their own stamp on the style. Look for Prairie, Craftsmen and Bungalow within this style.

L. Mission 1890-1920

In this style derived from the Spanish Missions of the Southwest, expect to see smooth stucco exteriors, low pitched tile roofs, overhanging eaves with exposed rafter ends, a gabled tile roof, enclosed courtyards, and arched entryways, arcades and windows.

M. Prairie Style 1890-1920

The Arthur B. & Maude Cooke House, Virginia Beach, VA

Frank Lloyd Wright's Falling Water 1959.

Using characteristic long low lines and natural elements Inspired by the broad, flat landscape of America's Midwest, the Prairie style was the first uniquely American architectural style. Frank LloydWright founded this style of home working from his Chicago studio. It reflects his beliefs that a structure should reflect and pay homage to the surrounding environment. The buildings feature horizontal rather than the vertical planes. The houses spread out over their lots, featuring flat or shallow hipped roof lines, rows of windows, overhanging eaves, and bands of stone, wood or brick across the surface. Prominent are the long low lines and natural elements. Interiors of these homes feature custom built-in furniture, low ceilings, massive central fireplaces, simple materials and open floor plans, which was a unique approach for the time.

N. Bungalow/Craftsman 1905-1930

The terms "craftsman" and "bungalow" are often used interchangeably, although there is a fundamental distinction. "Craftsman" refers generally to the Arts and Crafts movement and is considered an architectural or interior style, whereas "bungalow" is a particular form of house or building. Style details include low-pitched gable (triangular) roofs, walls clad in clapboard brick or stucco, overhanging eaves with exposed rafters and beams, heavy, tapered columns, patterned window panes and a covered front porch. In this style we see a typical color scheme emerge - roof colors are natural brown, green and red, complemented by an olive, dark green or russet body.

O. Kit homes

In the early 20th century, a unique opportunity arose for those seeking inexpensive homes. Sears Roebuck, Aladdin, Montgomery Ward and several other companies began to offer kit homes. Ordered from a catalog, these homes were shipped via rail car and arrived at the purchaser's building site complete with all material, even down to the nails and instructions for the completion. Each construction element was numbered to correspond to the detailed instructions for erecting the building. The plans available included every size and style the buyer could imagine and were also customizable to order. These homes are still found in towns across the country. Cape Charles, VA has several which are still being occupied and are often on tour. To identify an authentic kit home, it is necessary to inspect such items as the floor hoists and look for the number stamped on them at the factory.

NOTE: For further reading, Rebecca Hunter is an expert on these homes and has produced several books on the subject that are available from Amazon. To quote one of her books, she refers to "The house that came on the train". There are several publications of plans for these homes that can still be purchased. It is fascinating to look at the plans and see how efficient this concept was and how inexpensive.

P. Carpenter Gothic Revival 1840

Rufus Britt House circa 1910, Como, N C

Carpenter Gothic Revival houses, circa 1840, were influenced by the designs of architect and landscape designer Andrew Jackson Downing.   Buildings adopted a complex design that drew inspiration from symmetry and neoclassicism. Details included chimneys, gables, embrasure towers, warhead windows, gargoyles, stained glass and severely sloped roofs. Characteristics include hand sawn porch details, porcelain weathervanes, and fish scale shingles.

Q. Modern 1945-1965

Phillip Johnson Glass House c. 1949

Kaufman House c. 1946

As the twentieth century approached, preeminent architects Mies Van Der Rohe, Walter Gropius, and Frank Lloyd Wright were creating innovative new styles that featured less ornamentation, long low lines that reflected nature, and smaller footprints for homes.

Nearly all residential building ceased during years the country prepared for World War II. All resources were diverted to the war effort. After the war there was a greater need for smaller more affordable homes for the masses who wanted to get out of the cities. Suburban neighborhoods began to appear. Several distinctive styles evolved including ranch, shed roof, split levels.

Industrial and commercial properties also began to take on a new fresher look. The TWA Airlines Terminal is an example of more open floor plans, large glass expanses and sweeping roof lines.

TWA Flight Center, JFK Airport

California developer and builder Joseph Eichler was creating modernist styled homes in the 1950's and 60s'. He was the primary builder responsible for bringing modern homes to the masses, building over 11,000 homes. These homes are much sought after even today. They are thought of as works of art in many cases, and fetch the higher price to show for it.

Eichler, who himself lived in a Frank Lloyd Wright designed home, used many of Wright's design elements. His homes consisted of "front to back" planning- unheard of until this time. This style put all the living areas in the rear of the home. Fronts of the homes had small windows facing the street. The rear had very large windows that faced outdoor spaces. The construction was post and beam to allow for a more open floor plan. Front entries were small with views of the interior courtyard and carports were present for most. All his designs feature thin geometric roofs.

Adam Thoroughgood House Virginia Beach, VA

Clues to dating a House and tracing its history

An old house is not only the story of those who lived in it, a record of their tastes and achievements, it is a primary and irreplaceable part of the story of civilization. Marian Page author Historic Houses Restored and Preserved.

You have found that special house, and jumped through all of the legal and emotional hoops to be able to finally possess it. Now you would like to know more about it. How old is it? Who lived, loved and died here? Is it connected to anyone famous? How many brides floated down that magnificent staircase with butterflies in their tummies?

There are many resources to assist you in the hunt for information about your house.

The local tax assessor's office is a great place to start. There you can find the records of the purchases of your property beginning with yours and going back as far as the records go. Each of the previous owners will be listed along with what they paid for the property and generally a description of the property – did it have a house on it, barns, outbuildings, how big was the property? All these clues will lead you on toward locating old photos or wills, and probate records that can give you invaluable information and often lead you to surviving descendants. Since many of these records will have been recorded in the 18th century, you might need the assistance of a lawyer or title company employee who are experts at decoding tricky language on deed and title paperwork and the antique words and phrases that have fallen out of use.

The local or university library is also a good source. Many have a local history section that will be packed with photos and census information. Be aware that census takers in the 1800's had varying levels of education and could have gotten ages and names incorrect. But these records are a great source. The data collected from the 1800s and early 1900s includes information such as the names of all those living in a household at the time, their ages, occupations, places of birth. Some data is available for free on the U.S. Census web site (census.gov). There are fee-based services like Ancestry.com which offer pdf documents of census records to members. Also, check the Sanborn Insurance Maps of the area. This company has been in business since 1870. The maps contain all kinds of information that will be helpful in your search. And then, be sure to check out any local authors. They have personal insight into the history of structures and the families who lived in them in their area.

The library is also likely to have back issues of the local newspaper, which can provide you with tons of information. Hopefully, you will have the good luck to get a stack of dry old back issues handed to you; more likely, you'll have to scroll through rolls of microfilm, but the results will be worth it. It was the habit of small local papers to publish social details such as who attended whose wedding, dinner party, etc. They often covered the construction of new homes going up in the town, and may offer you information on where the builders got the materials used to build your house, why they made particular architectural design decisions, etc.

Once you've completed research to compile a comprehensive list of your home's past occupants and read up on their backgrounds through census records, you're ready to move on to the fun next step. Log on to the Internet and start hunting! Using Google and other search engines, look up any information you can find about the families who lived in your home and the surrounding streets, neighborhoods, and landmarks. Visit genealogy web sites to research prior owners as if they were your own relatives. Ask for help by putting questions on message boards. Don't forget to look at cemetery web sites. They offer ways to search for hard-to-find details about the people buried in them, such as maiden names and causes of death.

Note that date stones on old buildings are unreliable. They often are from other sites or an earlier building. People just never threw them away, and they were used many times as simple decoration.

The house itself will share all kinds of clues if you know what and how to look for them. But of course, only if you have been careful and not gutted every valuable piece of history out of it before you begin your hunt.

For instance, we were able to determine that the wrap around porch on our house in Murfreesboro, NC was added during the 1850 renovation done by A. G. Jones. How do we know that? From several tell-tale bits of information. For example, we know that the room added onto the house in 1900 as the town dentist office was added on after the porch. The original slanted porch flooring still exists under the current flooring of the room. We had to replace several pieces of flooring when renovating the room and were able to see the original porch floor.

One of the reasons we know that the renovation in 1850 was conducted by A. G Jones, who was a prominent architect of the time in Virginia and North Carolina, is that the fireplace mantel in the parlor bears his signature double column treatment. The North Carolina Department of History and Archives has been to the house to authenticate that he did indeed do the work, which includes the Greek Revival trim work on the window and door surrounds, the fireplace mantel, the double chestnut front doors, and unique lozenge shaped sidelights. Because all of the records for Hertford County were burned twice in the late 19th century, once by the Yankee forces and then again by an escaping prisoner from the jail, there are no existing records from that source. County tax records should be one of your first choices when researching the history of a property.

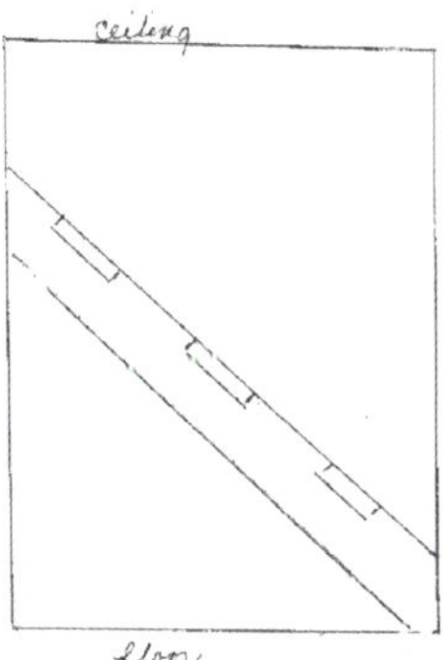

Another clue we discovered to determine that one section of our house is indeed 18th century construction was when we were recladding a wall in the back hallway. Inside the wall were existing beams set in on the diagonal rather than vertically. The beams each had slots cut into them that indicated that they were used for some other purpose at an earlier date. Since Murfreesboro was a shipping port in the 18th century, we feel these may have come from one of the old ships that called at the port and perhaps sunk nearby. It was very difficult to get supplies and lumber in those early days of settlement so these resourceful settlers used what they could get their hands on. One most power-ful clue that this is an 18th century building is that we know from records that there was a school on this property that taught native American children. It was run by a Reverend Burley, and was closed in 1796 just a few years before the house was built on the same site. We are fortunate in that this house is one of the few in the historic district that is on its original site. This adds to its historical significance and its contribution to the historic district.

Other physical clues to help date the structure include such items as the size of the wood used in the construction, the types of nails used, saw marks on timber, wall cladding, staircases, windows, door hardware, etc.

Before World War II, lumber was diametrically accurate. Two by fours were actually two inches by four inches. Modern lumber is "dressed" so that a quarter inch is planed off each side. Thus, a two by four is actually now 11/2" x 31/2".

Saw marks on timber can also be used to determine approximate dates of construction. It's important to understand that the use of axes, adzes, hand saws, manually-operat-ed pit saws, mechanical pit saws, and circular saws would have been used in overlap-ping eras. The earliest pit saws used a straight blade that moved in an alternating but straight line up and down - pulled and pushed by two workers: one standing on the log and another in the pit below the log, producing an X-type saw kerf (saw mark). The blades sometimes had a slight arc themselves, so even a pit saw blade kerf may not be dead straight, which left an acute X, and the cuts are not spaced at very regular inter-vals. Earliest use of circular saws is likely to appear on the Eastern Seaboard, probably in New England, as early as 1800 but were more commonly used throughout the eastern U.S. after about 1830. Early circular saw blades were small and were used to cut lath and framing studs; those leave a curve that has a smaller radius or a "sharper arc". Later saw blades were quite large. We have seen some several feet in diameter. These leave an arc with a much greater radius.

In the Colonial Period interior walls were generally wood. The walls were laid with wide boards hung vertically. Wainscoting was constructed of wide boards laid horizontally. Plaster or sheetrock, which do you have? Plaster walls involve a multi-stepped process of attaching lath boards to the studs, then applying several coats of plastering material, all of which have to dry before the next step can be applied.

Drywall (sheetrock) was invented in 1916 by the United States Gypsum Corporation to protect homes from urban fires, and marketed as the poor man's answer to plaster walls. Most of us call it by the brand name Sheetrock. Drywall did not catch on right away, but in the 1940s sales grew rapidly thanks to the baby boom.

18th century nails were handwrought on a forge and used often with wood pegs. They had square shanks and tapered to a point. From 1730-1836 cut nails began to be used. They were more uniform in shape with straight shanks and flat rectangular heads. By 1900, hand-made nails gave way to machine made wire nails with round tapering shanks and flat round heads.

Electrical wall switches are another indicator of construction. In 1890, Granville Woods created a push button dimmer switch that was used in theatres before gaining populari- ty in the home. Push-button switches were used from 1920-40.

Rotary snap type switches similar to this one pictured were used prior to that.

Brick bond patterns are invaluable in dating an older house. Three types; Flemish, American or common, and English (see Basic Terms in Appendices) were used from the 17th through the 18th century in the early colonies. In the 17th, 18th, and 19th centuries, most bricks were made by hand from clay and fired in brick clamps. These bricks had a courser texture than modern bricks and were softer. They were mortared with soft lime mortar, traditionally made from oyster shells. Though Portland cement was invented around 1824, it was not until around the turn of the 20th century that Portland cement and smoother, modern bricks began to replace the more traditional brick and mortar. Though it may take some practice, a trained eye can recognize the differences between hand-fired bricks and modern bricks; and lime mortar and modern cement. These details can provide additional clues for dating a building by the brickwork.

When you have completed all your research on your house, be sure to make it available for the next owner of the house and provide a copy to your local or state historical society and local library for their archives. All the information you have collected will be useful to others who are researching properties.

"Help Me Please", Elizabeth City, NC

Inspecting An Old Building

Older buildings require a much more thorough inspection than do newer homes. Many have no plumbing, electricity, or heat/ac systems that can be reused and therefore, dictate total replacement of these mechanical elements. And that can be ok depending on your skill set if you are planning to do much of the work yourself, and what your budget is. How much are you willing to invest in saving history?

It is always better to find a professional who knows about older buildings to assist you with your inspection, who will be licensed and insured, as well as knowledgeable. Just please do not purchase the house of your dreams and go into it and gut it without first doing a lot of planning. Think of all that will be lost to you if you take that route. Irreplaceable materials, beautiful crown moldings, wainscoting, leaded windows and all the stories that go with the house can never be replaced once they are gone. After all, aren't the details why you bought the house in the first place?

When searching for your perfect historic home, be sure to include a thorough inspection and consideration of the area in which it is located. We all know the old real estate saw – Location, Location, Location. It is as important when looking for an older home as it is with any real estate investment. We were lucky many years ago when we made our first historic house purchase. The town and historic commission were in the process of upgrading the historic district with new sewer piping, a hand-laid brick sidewalk, moving older houses into the area to save them and assisting home owners with their projects. Many of the houses were being renovated and restored by other owners like ourselves.

This is the kind of positive action you should hope to see. More recently we found a home we were interested in located in a town we knew to be progressive with their restoration policies. We decided that a personal look was warranted as the house had some lovely interior details and a good price through a revolving fund. We found the house located across a city street from a tumbled down and overgrown abandoned industrial complex. It was reached by an unpaved narrow lane, which in itself is not that bad. However, there were four other occupied buildings along the track. They were in abominable condition, needing extensive repairs.

These homes were in dire need of paint, the yards came complete with abandoned automobiles up on concrete blocks and furniture tossed into the yards. Not the kind of area to invest your time and considerable money even to save a worthwhile house - no wonder it is so attractively priced. A possible solution to saving this house would be to move it to a more suitable location, which of course adds several thousands of dollars to the cost of the investment.

Again, it comes down to how much you are willing to do and invest to save a home. If you consider moving a home to save it, a reputable house moving company with experience in older homes is a must. As always, do your due diligence to find the best mover available.

The areas that will need thorough inspection go from top to bottom and everything in between. Even if you are not doing the inspection yourself, you should be aware of what needs inspection.

<u>Exterior</u> –

Start with the <u>roofing materials</u>. Begin with a visual inspection of the exterior of the roof. If there is a sag in the ridge line, then you could have a major problem and may have to replace the ridge rafter itself a red flag that needs the expertise of an engineer to assess the probable costs. If you cannot access the roof itself, take along a good pair of binoculars to assist you as you inspect from the ground. Identify what you are working with and the condition of all its components – rafters, sheathing, moisture barrier, roof vents and of course, the roofing material. Many older homes still retain either their original cedar shakes or standing seam metal. Replacement of either is very expensive. A recent replacement of standing seam metal for one of our houses ran to $30,000. It was damaged in a hail storm, so thankfully insurance paid for it. Metal roofs usually last a minimum of 50 years if applied properly.

<u>Attic Space</u> – Inspect the underside of the roof sheathing. Is there evidence of leaking? If so, is it still viable or has rot set in? If so, then you will need to replace it when you redo the roofing material. Check out any insulation that is in the space. Many older homes do not have any, or not nearly enough, insulation in this area. Northern climes require considerably more insulation than the South. However, be mindful that you will need insula-

44

tion to keep the heat and cold from entering your living spaces even in the deep South.

<u>Exterior Walls</u> – Wood, brick, stone, or stucco? The type of cladding will react differently to the climate.

Wood walls can warp and become out of plumb, details may be missing or damaged, paint may be peeling, blistering or have mildew, eaves may be showing signs of leaking and rot.

Brick/Stone Construction This type of construction has its own set of problems. The brick can lose its mortar, and stone can break away or be of   stacked variety with no mortar between the stones.

<u>Windows/Doors</u> – Contrary to today's attitude of throwing away and replacing all windows in older homes, these old windows when properly maintained and restored are every bit as efficient as new ones - and the old ones will not become fodder for the landfill. Doors too can usually be repaired and refinished. Bear in mind, that these have been constructed of old growth wood which is much harder than today's products.

<u>Porches</u> -   Porches are the recipients of all the weather Mother Nature can throw at them. Rot can be rampant but repairable. Repair or replacement of rotted elements will be an important design part of the return of the building to its original condition.

<u>Foundation</u> – Foundations are the structures that hold the house up. They can be brick, stone or concrete piers, or in more modern homes it can be a poured concrete slab. If the floors in the house are uneven, you may need to do some work on these elements. Look at them closely, and if necessary, have a professional inspect them as these repairs can be very costly as well as dangerous to take on yourself.

<u>Crawl Space/Basement</u> – Crawl spaces tend to be confined and nasty spaces to inspect but you must know the condition of the foundation, floors, pipes, etc. so you can address any problems identified. Basements can exhibit leaking walls and floors that accumulate water after heavy rainfalls or snows. There are numerous solutions for these problems, but they can run into the thousands of dollars to repair.

<u>Interior</u>

<u>Ceilings</u> - Inspection of this element should be pretty straightforward. Does the ceiling sag? Are there signs of older leaks? Evidence of either of these may indicate that the material on the ceiling needs to be replaced. Another circumstance is that there are "dropped" ceilings. If so, will you be able to remove them to regain the original height of the ceilings. Often you will find the original ceiling material hidden above these later ceilings. Cross your fingers that you will find shiplap above.

<u>Walls Floors/Stairs</u> - Walls in many older homes will have wallcoverings ranging from painted canvas to uncoated wallpaper. If you plan to remove these, it usually involves labor intensive work. They can also be hiding deteriorating or damaged wall surfaces. Floors are most often covered in aged and dirty carpeting. However, older homes most usually had hardwood flooring in their original constructions. The uncovering and refinishing of these will restore the beauty of the house. If you watch HGTV or Magnolia's home shows, you will have seen someone roll a marble or ball across the floor to check how level it is. An uneven floor can mean that there is a problem with the foundation. Older homes may have settled over the years and will not always be level. The degree of settlement or damage can become expensive to repair. Stairs in older homes often are not up to today's codes of construction. They can be narrow or the steps are not uniform. This can mean a total replacement. Will there be room to expand the width and height? Perhaps because the house is older, the stairs will be grandfathered and you won't have to replace. These are questions for your inspector.

<u>Fireplaces</u> - Existing chimneys need to be thoroughly inspected by your professional. You may be lucky and find that all you need is a good chimney sweep to clean out any existing soot build up. The inspection should reveal whether or not there is internal damage to the flue. There are several options toward repairs if that is so - lining the flue with tile is one.

<u>Mechanical Systems</u> - The elements that make up the mechanics or workings of the house need to be inspected to insure they are safe, or if they need to be replaced. Look at the HVAC units if they are present. There may be no electric service to the house, but you still need to know what you are dealing with. Check the electrical systems, including the panel box. The minimum amount of power you need is 100 amps by code today. The recommended amperage is 200 considering all the appliances we are using as a norm in our homes today. Replacement of a panel box can be very costly but certainly this is the time to replace it. A homeowner should expect to pay between $750 and $2,000 to upgrade an existing unit to a 200-amp service, including professional install.

Many older homes will still have what is known as "Knob and Tube" wiring. This was a technique used in the US from 1830 to about 1940. If the wiring has been maintained properly, you may be able to reuse it. However, you will run into considerable resistance from your homeowner's insurance company, so it is better to rewire the property for long term efficiency.

Plumbing - Depending on the age and condition of the house you are considering, the plumbing may be in poor repair or non-existent. Old cast iron piping needs to be replaced. Over the years corrosives will have accumulated inside the pipes, reducing the flow of water and may well contain contaminates that will cause illness. It is wiser to include replacement of piping in your budget. Often you can recycle existing fixtures. Old cast iron tubs and sinks are hard to replace in terms of design and function. If the surfaces are damaged or stained, they can be refinished and you will have a real prize.

Water Heaters – These items should also be replaced unless they are relatively new (five to six years old). While the plumber is re-piping, he will need to re-pipe the water heater as well to use the newest products. You might as well go all the way and put in a newer more energy efficient and reliable heater unit while he is there. Then you know you will not wake up some morning to find your newly refinished floor flooded.

Site/Landscaping - Landscaping is a vital element for the completion of a project. Many times, those overgrown and leggy existing plants can be moved to a better location, trimmed back, fed and they become a new and better contributing factor to the overall look of the property. Trees can be "limbed up" to allow more light into the structure. Trimming vegetation also eliminates or lessens damage to the roof, walls, and trim of the house.

The Inspection: An initial inspection to determine whether or not the building is in a condition you can work with is one of the first things you must do. If you have decided on the property, then it will be well worth the expenditure to hire a good home inspector who is trained to look for pitfalls and dangers in these old structures before your actual purchase. If you plan to be present when the inspection is being done, come prepared to get your hands dirty. When going to inspect a structure there are tools that will aid you in determining the condition of the house. Always bring along a good camera, the best flashlight you can find, an awl to test the condition of wood, a measuring tape and a circuit tester, paper and pen. If the house is particularly in bad shape or overgrown with vegetation, remember to wear a hard hat and gloves and stout shoes and clothes that can be thoroughly washed after you are done. Abandoned houses tend to become the living quarters of all kinds of critters – bats, snakes, cats. etc. It is not a good idea to go into an abandoned place alone. Many of these old houses are infested with fleas so take some bug spray to put on your arms and legs. No sense taking those nasty critters back to your home at the end of the day.

While you are selecting your team to work with you toward your project, what is called your "brain trust", do your due diligence and research to be sure you are hiring craftspeople with the same love for old houses that you have. I know of an architect who has a contract with a local city to rehab the houses in a wonderful old early 20th century neighborhood with lovely Victorian era homes of various sizes and styles. It was developed as a "Streetcar" Community so that residents could commute to nearby employment at naval shipyards. When this person's crew gets done, there is so little left of the original you would not know they are old houses. He also builds "infill" houses, newly constructed houses that echo the styles of the originals, for those too far gone to save. You cannot tell which is which. He totally guts the property and has everything carried off to the local land fill. All the old growth lumber, random width wood floors, cornices, door frames, and beautiful leaded glass windows - lost forever. I suggested to him that he contact a local salvage yard or Habitat for Humanity Restore to have them collect the things for reuse. His response was – I do not have time for that. Really?   This is also an example of how a municipality and historic organizations can lose control of the work being conducted in their town. Stricter inspections and control should have been exercised here. Why have all the covenants and restrictions in place if they are not going to be rigorously enforced?

You may run into those with this biased attitude on your journey. Choose very carefully when you select an architect, designer and contractor. Be sure they have experience in renovating old houses and more importantly, that they have a deep respect and even love for them. Be sure they work harmoniously together as a solid team.

Once the property has been inspected and detailed plans readied (the more detailed the better), document everything.   Take the time to do a thorough survey of every room, measure every room, take tons of photos of every element of the interior and the exterior. Also take lots of pictures of the streetscape around the house. Compile a notebook with all your ideas and plans, photos, etc. It will become your bible during the time the work is being done. If the house is significant enough to warrant listing on the National Register of Historic Places, you will need to have all these elements in place to complete the registration forms.

After this preparation work is completed, you are finally ready to begin the most satisfying, and admittedly the most grueling, phase. All that is left is….. “the work”.

Tax Credits and Tax Exemptions for Historic Preservation

We do have a struggle when historic preservation is involved.   Allen Etter

Myriad tax incentives exist at the local, state, and federal levels to encourage responsible citizens to take on the costs of purchase and upkeep of historic property and promote investment in local economies.

Historic Tax credits are state enabled incentives. There are strict guidelines as to what qualifies a property – purchase price does not qualify, but the cost to rehabilitate does. All tax credits are modeled after the guidelines in Section 47 of the US Internal Revenue Service tax code.

Twenty-eight states currently offer owners of historic properties the use of tax credits, and while the ordinances and restrictions may vary from state to state these credits can make the purchase of the property more affordable in terms of the rehabilitation that is done. Generally, the guidelines are much the same - the five criteria do not vary. They are: which property qualifies, detailed standards to follow, a minimum threshold of investment, methods of calculating the value of the credit applied for, and the body who governs the process. Applicants may be eligible for tax credits for rehabilitation work on properties that are listed in the National Register of Historic Places, or are certified as contributing to a listed historic district. The rehabilitation work must meet the <u>Secretary of the Interior's Standards for Rehabilitation</u> developed by the National Park Service. (A copy of the Standards and Guidelines for some states are included in the Appendix for your convenience.)

For owners of income producing historic properties, there are also federal rehabilitation tax credits. The federal program is managed by the National Park Service, but applications are first submitted to the State Historic Preservation Office (located within the Division of Historical and Cultural Affairs) for review. Once your site is a designated historic property, you may be eligible for as much as 20% credit for repairs you make on that property. If you are renovating your home and include home office space or rent out space, then you may also be eligible for the tax credit. If you are operating a bed and breakfast, you will be eligible.

One example of the information available to home owners is this quote from the NC State Historic Preservation Office (SHPO) ncdcr.gov. "Income tax incentives for the rehabilitation of historic structures are important tools for historic preservation and economic development in North Carolina. A federal income tax credit for the rehabilitation of historic structures first appeared in 1976 and today consists of a 20% credit for the qualifying rehabilitation of income-producing historic properties. Since 1976, over 3,100 completed "certified rehabilitation" projects have been reviewed by the N.C. State Historic Preservation Office, representing almost two billion dollars of investment in historic properties. The spinoff from all this activity includes job creation, downtown and neighborhood revitalization, improved community appearance, and greater community pride. Historic preservation is smart growth, and smart investment."

Many localities also provide programs of tax exemptions for historic properties. Working with your local historical preservation office, main street revitalization group or historical society, you may be able to work out a "tax deferment" on property tax increases. These deferments usually last as many as 10 to 15 years, and they are based on plans to renovate your historical property or a promise to keep said property as-is without significantly altering its character. In other words, your property taxes will remain based on the value of the property when you purchased it for the period of the freeze. Once the freeze period is exhausted, the property will be reassessed and a new tax rate levied. Contact your local tax assessor's office to explore this option.

The Mary Smith House protected by the Historic Charleston Foundation

Owners of historic properties know and recognize that those structures and their surroundings are fragile and irreplaceable. How can the owners best protect the property for the long term?   There are several methods that will ensure that the property is not destroyed and replaced by a big box store, with seemingly miles of ugly tarmac covered parking lots.

Of course, you will purchase a homeowners insurance policy for the property. Be aware there are considerations here that are not readily apparent and need to be investigated. "Replacement value" does not necessarily apply when the insured home is an historic property. By today's standards, replacement coverage often means the insurer will only reimburse you for 125% of the amount of your policy. That may allow you to walk away from the damaged or destroyed property with enough money to purchase a new home. However, it may not be enough to rebuild the house with the irreplaceable materials it once had. It is wiser to acquire a Replacement Rider which will assure that the proper materials can be used to return the property to its original state. There are insurers who target older properties such as Chubb Group or Fireman's Fund.   These policies will cost you more, but they will also guarantee replacement cost.   You will be able to restore your home with the wide-plank hardwood flooring or hand-glazed tiles for your fireplace.

Two terms most used in relation to protecting historic properties are easements and covenants. Both can be affirmative or negative. However, easements are typically affirmative, giving the holder the right to use the servient land, whereas covenants are typically negative, limiting what the burdened party can do on her own land. Servient land is defined as real property which has an easement or other use imposed upon it in favor of another property (called the «dominant estate»), such as right of way, or use for access to an adjoining property or utility lines.

An appealing useful legal tool for many property owners is the historic preservation easement. What is this and how does it protect the property? First it is a voluntary legal agreement, typically in the form of a deed, which permanently protects a significant historic property. It restricts the current and future use of the property that is entered into by the owner of the property and a qualified preservation organization or agency. In the agreement the property owner promises to continue to protect the property's historic integrity. Specific items can include: required proper maintenance, no inappropriate additions, alterations or demolition. The organization is given the right to enforce the agreed upon covenants of the easement, and to monitor the property to insure those are followed. Within the agreement, the owner retains the right and duty to manage and care for the property as set forth in the agreement, and must pay the property taxes in full and on time. He also retains the right to continue to live in the property as long as he wishes and can sell, lease or pass on the property to his heirs. An owner who donates an historic preservation easement may be eligible for one or more forms of tax benefits.

Preservation easements are meant to be flexible tools used to ensure that the historic resources of a property are enforced. They are also meant to be custom-designed to meet the needs of the homeowner. Easements can protect the exterior of the buildings, or both the exterior and interior. Interior easements are rare and when in place still may only protect a part of the interior. It is more difficult to monitor and review interior spaces that are held in private ownership. The landscape can also be protected by an easement when it is deemed historically significant.

There are some costs involved for the property owner when committing to a historic preservation easement. He will be required to pay for the title search on the property, any land surveys required, fees for appraisals and usually any accounting fees related to the transaction. Some organizations request a financial donation referred to as a "stewardship fee".

While the duration of the easement is mutually agreed upon by the owner and the agency and decided during the negotiation, the terms of the easement are not easily altered once it is in place. It is meant to be a long-term commitment by the owner to preserve and conserve the property. It can only be altered by mutual agreement of all parties of the agreement. If the owner wishes to claim income or estate benefits, it must be made in perpetuity.   All easements are governed by state property laws and can vary from state to state. Twenty-two states, the District of Columbia, Puerto Rico and the U.S. Virgin Islands have adopted the Uniform Conservation Easement Act. To learn more about this valuable preservation tool, see www.nccusl.org

Interior easements protect significant historic interiors. They usually cover the primary rooms of a house with high historic integrity. They do not typically protect kitchens or bathrooms. Pictured is 59 Church Street, Charleston, SC

Periodic Maintenance of Historic Structures

Watch an old building with anxious care, guard it as bet you may, and at any cost, from very influence of dilapidation.   John Ruskin, The Seven Lamps of Architecture, 1848

Once we recognize that we, as historic house owners, are only the stewards of these pieces of history, we realize that we must preserve and maintain them. A critical element of preservation of historic structures is maintenance – diligent, skilled, and thorough. Without constant maintenance and vigilance, a historic building begins to lose its integrity and begins a decline which is difficult if not impossible to halt or reverse.

Owners of older homes or commercial buildings must develop periodic maintenance plans which address and repair areas of neglect on a cyclical basis. A plan puts you in control of what is happening to your building instead of only reacting when a serious issue presents itself. It is less costly and more effective in the long run to stay ahead of these issues as they arise.   Effective maintenance is mostly doing the right thing at the right time, and a well thought out written plan allows you to recognize the areas of concern on a regular schedule. It is a continuing process, and cannot be approached as a one-time task to be done and forgotten. Damaged parts can be repaired or replaced, if necessary, but only up to a certain point of decay and neglect.

All building materials deteriorate, some at a much faster rate than others. Wood, even when painted, will degrade within a few years while masonry may take decades to show appreciable wear. As wear takes place, the materials will need care and maintenance. An awareness of just how often and how much maintenance is required is invaluable to the home owner. A comprehensive plan with diligent inspections is key to the longevity of an historic property.

Roger Reed of the Maine Historic Preservation Commission has summed up the two basic reasons for maintaining the existent parts rather than replacing them. He says, "The practical reason is that maintenance is more efficient. It saves money, time, and effort by limiting the need for future expensive work. It is less costly and more efficient to fix a window than it is to wait for it to become so deteriorated that wholesale replacement is needed. Moreover, replacement material is often inferior to the original. For example, modern slow-growth wood is generally inferior to the old slow-growth wood used in old building. Maintaining the original wood makes sense because it is less prone to deterioration."

He adds, "The philosophical reason is that historic buildings are an important part of our heritage. Frequently, our homes and institutional buildings such as churches, are the most powerful ties we have to our past. They are historic only insofar as the materials they are made of are old. That is what distinguishes an historic building from a replica and why we maintain and preserve the historic fabric of a building for future generations. Maintaining the original parts preserve the building's historic integrity."

You must plan to maintain your historic property, while honoring its unique characteristics and the materials used to construct it originally.

When developing a maintenance plan, it is essential that you include the following elements: how often you will inspect the property for maintenance issues, a checklist that becomes a record of all repairs/maintenance conducted on the property, and identification of which of the components will require professional repairs. These components become a checklist for you to use as your guideline for doing inspections and repairs. As an example, roofing materials, chimneys and eaves, guttering and downspouts can be inspected from the ground with binoculars every six months; flashing, exterior walls and painted surfaces can be inspected every twelve months.

Start from ground level and closely examine each elevation of the building using your checklist. Be careful when inspecting that you do not damage eaves and gutters by propping your ladder against them. Steep slippery roof surfaces can be dangerous and shingles can be damaged by walking on them so tread carefully. Wear gloves and protective eyewear as necessary while conducting your inspection. Difficult areas may need to be inspected by professionals.

There is a sample of a checklist included in the Appendices for your use.

Greenhabbing Your Historic Property

"Plenty of cities have areas in them that we would characterize as suburban and should be retrofitted, and plenty of municipalities that we think of as suburban still have those remnants of a little old main street, a couple of blocks of great urban bones that should be expanded upon," says author Ellen Dunham-Jones.

We have talked a great deal about the why's and how's of retrofitting historic properties. To get down to more specific information, this method of preserving our history is a way to reclaim a property with the environment in the forefront of the work. According to studies made by the Building Materials Reuse Association, construction and demolition waste is the largest single-stream source of refuse in the United States - more than double the amount thrown into household trash bins.

What is Greenhabbing? Greenhabbing or green rehabbing (eco-friendly, energy-efficient, sustainable, etc.) means taking older homes and renovating them so that they are well-insulated and air-sealed, have high-efficiency HVAC equipment, manage moisture and drainage properly, and feature some sustainable aspects, such as recycled materials used in flooring or cabinets/counter tops, etc.

An English architect friend of mine related the story of how he restored his stone farmhouse which was built in the 16th century. The walls of the house are three feet thick made with large stones and all of the cavities were filled with dried dung as insulation. So even as early as this, the builder understood the importance of having air tight walls to keep the cold out. This house is built on a headland so it gets a tremendous amount of harsh wind in the winter. The roof, a type known as a "Gravity Roof" was built with locally quarried slate in two and a half feet by three feet one-inch-thick sizes. It was held down with hand cut oak pegs laid down on hard wood timber strips. He knows this first hand as he removed each slate tile, cleaned it and then turned it to the other side and replaced it on the roof. Can you even begin to imagine how heavy the roof is on that house? It needed huge thick stone walls just to support the roof.

Greenhabbing a property involves making improvements that reduce its environmental impact and lower its overall operating costs. What does this mean for historic properties? You will be surprised how easy it is to add "green elements" into your rehab while keeping the charm and value of the period. Below is a list of some of the basic greening tips you can use in your projects which protect the environment.

Use as much recycled material as is available either from your own   demolition, or resources such as Habitat ReStore or salvage yards. Also include products that are recyclable so that when the house is remodeled in the future, those can be reused again even decades later. Conversely, make an effort to recycle everything that you can during the course of your project. There are lots of folks who will be happy to have what you no longer need. Check your area Habitat Restore, local architectural salvage yards, or even advertise your items for sale in your local paper. The Building Materials Association can also be a good resource.Go solar or not? That will depend largely on whether or not your historic house is in a designated historical district and what the restrictions are within it. Since the emphasis is now on the saving of historic properties and ensuring their survival, more and more historical associations are rethinking those restrictions and including allowances for the installation of solar panels within reason. If your house is within a district, check with the governing body to see what they will allow before going to the considerable expense of purchasing and installing the system. Some solar roof tiles can be supplied in Solar PV for better more aesthetic appearance. Consult your solar provider for advice on what is the newest technology available, as improvements are being made rapidly.

Use paints that are either Low VOC, No VOC or All Natural. All older paints can contain Volatile Organic Compounds (VOC) that release a potent gaseous odor when first applied. Low-VOC or no-VOC paints are odor-free and won't compromise air quality. Most paint companies now produce these paints for use. Natural products such as Milk Paint, which uses milk proteins as a binder, is popular because it is durable. It will have a slight texture and will necessitate more planning and prep work Install low-flow plumbing. Most old houses need a plumbing upgrade at some point, and that is your golden opportunity to make it green! Low-flow plumbing uses much less water, thus helping the environment while keeping your water bills down. Many municipalities offer a rebate when you install new low-flow toilets. When replacing or repairing floors in your house, opt for reclaimed hardwoods rather than new products. It will have inherent charm, history and beauty just like the house you so carefully chose, and it will save trees.

Rather than use fiberglass, use cellulose for insulation. Cellulose is made from recycled newspapers which are mixed with boric acid. It has a very low carbon footprint and works just as well as fiberglass. Another option is the products produced by ROCKWOOL (www.rockwool.com). Their unique products, made of stone and other recycled materials, repel water so R-value is not affected. They are also completely resistant to rot, mildew, mold, and bacterial growth, contributing to a safer indoor environment in your home. They provide indoor comfort in summer and winter, and help reduce heating and cooling costs. These energy savings also translate into reduced CO2 emissions.

Since this is an historic house, you may want to find and reuse antique lighting fixtures. Consult your local lighting codes. The good news is that today we are able to source bulbs that will work in these older fixtures. Reproduction Edison bulbs are available in numerous sizes and wattages. Fixtures themselves are available in salvage yards and on Facebook from sources such as Historic Architectural Salvage Market. Individuals post their unique products on this site at reasonable prices.

Many have already been restored.

Instead of replacing and disposing of your old windows, repair them as often as possible. It is a fact that it takes 126% more energy to produce new aluminum/vinyl units than it does to repair existing ones. Preserve them by replacing crumbling caulk, repairing the frames, and repainting. The idea that they will not be as energy efficient as newer windows is a myth and you will avoid taking them to a landfill. Only 10% of heat loss is caused by windows. The rest exits through the roof of the home. So, it is better to add additional insulation in the attic, walls and under floors to increase R-values. Keeping existing windows will also retain more of the original character of the property.

Kitchen countertops are another good opportunity to go green. There are numerous products on the market today that work well. Butcher block, both naturals and manufactured stone products, recycled glass, concrete, metal and laminates offer the homeowner a vast variety of choices.

When hiring a contractor look for one who is a qualified green professional. Is he aware of the newest and best technology? Does he understand the terms of being a LEED (Leadership in Energy and Environmental Design) project? The Green Home Guide, a service of the U.S. Green Building Council will help you greatly.

Avoid using harsh chemicals during your remodeling work as much as possible. Sometimes, it is necessary to use chemicals for such areas as old oil paint removal. However, you should try to use products that are gentle on the environment and your health.

It may seem to be a very ambitious goal to achieve a net-zero lifestyle for those of us who are remodeling older homes. But, if we are to stand any chance against climate catastrophe, architects, engineers, and the buildings they create will necessarily have to assume a larger role in moving us toward a better environment. This movement cannot be one only in creating shiny new buildings, but much more crucially, by retrofitting our existing structures.

Energy efficiency is a key factor in reducing emissions and curbing the effects of climate change. Residential and commercial buildings alone accounted for about 39% of total energy consumption last year in the U.S., according to the Environmental and Energy Study Institute, and a recent report from the UN found that 65% of projected building stock expected worldwide in 2060 has already been built.

We need to act to improve our existing structures—and quickly. Old buildings can, and should also be sustainable buildings. Although LEED certification is often associated with modern new office towers, in fact, some of our oldest structures benefit the most from sustainability upgrades. Increasing energy efficiency and reducing carbon impact is an imperative in today's world. This does not mean that historic buildings must lose their unique architectural features, nor their cultural context within the community. Historic structures can readily enhance their energy efficiency, the quality of indoor air and other features through obtaining LEED certification. These historic buildings represent continuity, and the importance of knowing where we came from. Their careful preservation ensures that the places from our past will continue to support future generations.

The LEED projects below show how we can support places with historic or cultural value, and still make them into healthy and efficient spaces in which to work and learn.

Sede Centrale, headquarters for Ca' Foscari University of Venice, is the oldest LEED-certified building on the planet (556 years old).

The previous record holder, Fay House at Radcliffe Institute for Advanced Study, Harvard University, circa 1807 was built as a private residence. In 1885 it became the first permanent building for Radcliffe College.

Photo by Kevin Grady

Like its historic neighbors, the headquarters of the Harvard Center for Green Buildings and Cities is covered in shingles and has an inviting front porch. Impossible to miss, however, are the modern bits -solar panels and angular gray window shades - which hint at the innovation happening inside.

See Appendices for information on LEED certification, and additional information and resources.

Pythian Hall, Portsmouth, VA

Adaptive Reuse of Historic Structures

This process is the recycling and repurposing of historic buildings. In other words, using an old site or building for a purpose other than that for which it was built. This urban planning method is a vehicle for reversing the trends of decline for structures which have fallen behind in our fast-paced sprawling development style. The reuse of old buildings is the ultimate in recycling. Having already withstood the test of time, these old buildings structures are ripe for adaption to new uses. Rather than just bulldoze a significant building, those interested in preservation much prefer alternatives such as restoration of original exterior features and adaptation of the interior for a different purpose. To quote Myrick Howard, President of Preservation North Carolina, "There are few activities that are more job-intensive and return more dollars to the local economy that historic rehabilitation. You can't outsource renovation. Returning a historic building to new utility requires more labor and higher skills than new construction, and more money is pumped back into the community. It just makes so much sense to reuse our historic buildings."

Some interesting statistics - things to think about: from an article "Reuse of Historic Buildings to Address Climate Change" by Linda Reeder. AIA: It takes an incredible amount of energy to construct a new building. As a group, buildings constructed before 1920 are more energy efficient than those constructed from 1920 through 1999. Removal of these existing buildings adds literally tons of waste to our landfills. The demolition of a 50,000 square foot building creates 4,000 tons of debris - enough to fill 26 railroad cars or a train nearly a quarter of a mile long. These dense old-growth materials are irreplaceable- wide plank flooring, windows with hand crafted glass, hand crafted moldings, stained glass. Even old windows can be restored and are as energy efficient as the unsightly new vinyl ones. Not to mention that we are losing the last vestiges of the work of regionally or nationally famed architects.

Currently we are seeing a renewed interest in this process, but it is not a new concept. Rather, it is one that is centuries old. One of the oldest examples is the Temple of Antoninus and Faustina within the Roman Forum. The temple was originally built in 140 AD as a monument to Antoninus's deceased wife Faustina. It has had many incarnations since that time and most of them religious. It was converted to Roman Catholic in 7th Century and then became Universitas Aromatorium in 1429 (College of Chemists and Herbalists). It is still sometimes open to the public and contains notable artworks. There is a university museum and archive next door. Thousands of years of continuous use from a single structure.

The Tate Modern Museum, London, England

Another very recognizable and successful example of reuse is the Tate Modern Gallery in London. This building began its life as the Bankside Power Station. The power station closed in 1981 & reopened in 2006 as Tate Modern. There are various galleries in the large space. The 5 story Turbine Hall which formerly housed electric generators, and the Tanks – 3 large underground oil tanks have been refurbished into galleries. Formerly off-limits to the public as the Power Station, it now serves nearly five million visitors a year.

We can all bring to mind an old church conversion, a chic restaurant in an old factory, a quaint bed and breakfast in a magnificent old home, a warehouse district that now hosts wonderful boutiques and art galleries, or a small house museum.

One exciting new trend in our center city districts as they become "reurbanized", is the conversion of large commercial or religious sites becoming loft apartments for the influx of millennials born between 1980 and 1997 who want to live in the heart of the action. This group is the largest and most diverse generation in the country's history. Millennials seek varied authentic experiences, and old and historic places fill the bill for them. They want the convenience of being able to walk to restaurants, shops and entertainment venues. Since they are so environmentally aware, they want a smaller carbon footprint and to be able to walk, bike or take public transportation to work every day. Reclaiming city streets and making them more amenable to walking and mass transit helps neighborhoods thrive again.

In several cities the large churches that are no longer in use are being converted to chic apartments. One example is Sanctuary Lofts in Philadelphia. Located in the 180-year-old Greater St. Matthew Baptist Church, it is Philadelphia's first church conversion into loft-style rental apartments. Each brand-new loft residence boasts distinctive design elements from this re-imagined church, ranging from "cathedral ceilings", (no pun intended), to restored stained glass window treatments. Old world craftsmanship blends with contemporary design, sophisticated European-styled cabinetry, and stainless-steel appliances.

I recently conducted a walking tour of downtown Norfolk, VA which has seen a huge increase in conversion of its historic district. We were fortunate to have a representative of the development corporation which has done most of the work accompany us on the tour. What a treat to see these wonderful old hotels, a former Navy YMCA, and a large office building in their new guises.

The Wainwright Building, Norfolk, VA

The Wainwright Building in the Freemason Historic District began its life as the head-quarters for the Seaboard Air Line Railway. Built in 1925-1926, the nine-story, 92,000 square-foot, steel reinforced concrete building is "V"-shaped and faced in textured yellow brick with numerous stone decorative elements in the Late Gothic Revival style. The main entrance and lobby are the highlight of the interior with nearly all of the historic features intact including a ribbed vaulted ceiling, a large completely brass entry wall and doors, and granite walls and flooring.

Main Lobby of the Wainwright Building, Norfolk, VA

The Rockefeller, formerly the Navy YMCA, Norfolk, VA

The Rockefeller, formerly the Navy YMCA, Norfolk. VA Restored Exterior Main Staircase

The Rockefeller, the former Navy YMCA donated to Norfolk by John D. Rockefeller and known for many years as the Union Mission, has an incredible lobby restored to its original elegance. The railings on the lobby staircase are carved wood, not wrought iron and the floors are marble. Can you image the craftsmanship that it took to do these? Apartments were carefully placed to retain many of the original hand painted murals, the gym floor with its basketball markings, etc. This building recently won a very prestigious award for Design Excellence, as I am sure you can understand.

Three of the hotels which were constructed to support the Jamestown Exhibition in 1906 have been beautifully converted to residential use while retaining their original mosaic patterned tile floors, marble walls, brass elevator doors, etc.

Formerly the James Madison Hotel circa 1906 now The Hames Apartments Norfolk, VA

Freemason Abbey, built in 1873 also stands in downtown Norfolk, still an active part of the culture. Thanks to the vision of developer Jerry Collier, who saw the potential of a dilapidated structure in need of repair in 1987, the former church conversion was conceived. This vision was transformed into reality and once again the building feels new, exciting and full of life as a meeting place for all to enjoy. How appropriate that many couples become engaged over dinner or celebrate a rehearsal dinner in the former church.

Why should we save and reuse these old structures? In the case of inner-city areas, they are already a vital part of the cityscape, integrated into the existing architectural landscape. Removing them not only is very costly but once a building is gone, often the replacement costs are so great that space never gets in-filled and it soon becomes a blight on the area with increasing crime making it no longer safe for the inhabitants. To quote David J. Brown, Chief Preservation Officer of the National Trust, "Future generations deserve to be able to immerse themselves in this rich story we all share."

Many "sustainable features" can be found in historic buildings. Although this term is relatively new to come into use, these include passive heating and cooling as a result of site orientation and natural ventilation, natural daylight, and use of durable local materials. This concept extends too into regional architectural treatments of buildings. As we know, buildings in the South sport taller ceilings, larger and more windows that allow better air circulation - all in a bow to the higher temperatures and humidity. In the Northern areas of the country, buildings tend to have lower ceilings and fewer windows in order to retain heat. Reusing existing buildings saves energy by avoiding new construction and diverts demolition waste from landfills. New construction increases greenhouse gas emissions considerably. "The greenest building is the one already built," as Carl Elefante, AIA, says, is a concept embraced by the National Trust for Historic Preservation (NTHP).

Some Federal and State Tax Credits are still available for restoration and renovation projects, making it easier for owners to save these pieces of history. Every state maintains a State Historic Preservation Office (SHPO) which can provide interested persons with application forms and detailed information regarding the process. A list of several and their contact information is provided in the Appendix.

While this is a lengthy and complicated process (one friend likened it to a Masters dissertation), it is well worth the effort required. In the case of large commercial buildings, the process is even more protracted. Such issues as the original lengths and breath of hallways, door placement and original materials determine the sizes of apartments and rooms, window replacement or retention, etc.

Main Street, Murfreesboro, NC

We are fortunate that many small "main street" towns have recognized the potential of revitalizing their downtown areas. Main Streets are the core of the community and the traditional center for cultural, social and economic activities. No more abandoned boarded up buildings. Instead, they are once again hubs for business and are revenue producing centers of activity. Cape Charles, VA, Titusville, FL, Laurel, MD, and Smithfield, VA, Franklin, VA, and Edenton, NC to name just a few, all have wonderful shops, trendy cafes and accommodations to draw tourists. These tourist dollars refill the town coffers with needed funds in the form of taxes generated by local businesses, and increase local employment while providing enjoyment for those who visit. I was asked to assist Titusville FL in hosting an event showcasing the shops on historic Washington Street, to acquaint and educate the public in learning why we should preserve our built environment. The event included a walking tour and my lecture on Adaptive Reuse. Participants discovered that restaurants, breweries and galleries have replaced many of the old businesses. These new businesses serve to draw locals as well as tourists downtown and revitalize the area with new money and interest.

I have had the privilege to work closely with the director of the historic Pritchard House in Titusville, FL. This historic house museum allows visitors an opportunity to experience the furnishings, accessories and lifestyle of the early 20th century in Titusville. A cherished professional privilege for me was to meet Mary Schuster who lived her entire life in this house. When I talked to her, she had just celebrated her 100th birthday. She was a lovely Southern lady and I know she is missed in Titusville. These are the kinds of experiences and memories that are available only because of the foresight and labor of those who save these structures, and open them to the public for visitation.

Before The Pritchard House, Titusville, FL Restored

Let us look at some of the other projects that have recently been completed around the country. There are many unique projects involving the Adaptive Reuse process that are worth mention.

The Vendue, one of the first boutique art hotels in the country, is located in the heart of Charleston's historic French Quarter Art District. This series of buildings began their lives as warehouses in 1785. The name refers to the "vendue masters" or auctioneers who worked in the area. During the Civil War, the buildings became warehouses for blockade runners. Later they evolved into warehouses for the fishing industry. Purchased in 2012 by Avocet Hospitality who completed a $5.5 million renovation, the hotel reopened in 2014. The public areas of the hotel serve as an ever-changing art gallery with works from local artists. The current owner retained a portion of the building that once served as the offices of the South Carolina Gazette, operated by the first female newspaper publisher in the US. Today, with a gracious bow to its past, its known as "The Press", serving Starbucks coffees and snacks.

The Craddock-Terry Hotel in Lynchburg, VA is the former Craddock-Terry Shoe Company. Begun in 1888, It grew to be the fifth largest shoe manufacturer in the world and was the only shoe factory below the Mason-Dixon line making 100,000 pair per day at its peak. The company held contracts with the government to manufacture boots for soldiers. The current owner is the great grandson of John W. Craddock who started the company, located on the banks of the James River. It took nearly five years to restore the two buildings including having to replace the entire roof system. Today it is a wonderful boutique hotel on the bluff above the James River. Included in the interior design of the hotel are shoe motifs such as the room designations, a wonderful shoe chaise in the lobby. Your continental breakfast can be served in your room in a reproduction shoe-shine box. And if you are lucky, you may even get to meet the hotel dog, Penny.

The Hotel Emma in downtown San Antonio, TX has had a very interesting history. It is now a very chic boutique hotel, but it began its life as Pearl's Brewhouse in 1894. The hotel is named in honor of Emma Koehler who ran the brewery after the death of her husband, the founder, in 1914, through the Prohibition years until 1933. There were in fact three Emma's who were connected to the building. Emma Koehler, a nurse called Emmi, who was hired to help her after an accident in 1910, and Emmi's tall blonde friend also named Emma. Apparently, Mr. Koehler had an affinity for ladies named Emma. He had affairs with both Emmi and the tall blonde Emma, setting them up in a house in town for his convenience no doubt. After an argument in the wee hours in November 1914, blonde Emma shot him to death. She was subsequently found not guilty by an all-male jury. Such were the times. What a story to share with today's guests!

The Arcade Providence, the nation's oldest indoor shopping mall built in 1828 in the historic heart of Providence, RI, has recently undergone a major renovation creating retail space on the ground floor, and 45 micro-living condos on the second and third floors. The condos range from 225-800 square feet but include all the modern amenities.

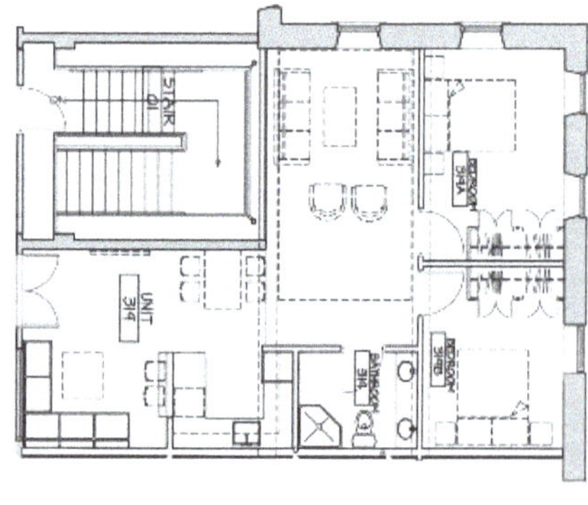

UNIT 319

Another interesting project is one located in the historic heart of Uptown Charlotte, NC. The building was constructed in 1927 as a 20-story bank. Now known as Tryon Plaza, the new owners have successfully converted the building

into office condominiums. During the restoration, they retained as many of the original Art Deco elements as possible. The original elevator bank and doors were restored. The Executive Board Room, which is part of the conference center for the building, still retains its original paneling, gorgeous hand-crafted glass chandelier and beautifully patterned wood floors. The amazing sandstone archway which was adorned with intricate carvings by Italian artisans, still welcomes visitors and owners to the building. Elegant hallways give way to thoroughly modern amenities including a conference center, concierge service, owner's lounge fitness center and generous storage units.

Savannah GA's Art Moderne style Greyhound bus station built in 1938 is enjoying a rebirth as a fine dining restaurant called "The Grey". New owners retained its porthole windows and terrazzo flooring, including the well-worn spot in front of the former ticket window. A replica of the blue and white Vitrolite exterior involved labor-intensive hand cutting and installation of the glass. Its Southern influenced menu has received national attention.

A five story former Farmers & Merchants Bank that opened in 1924 in Kinston, NC has been converted to The O'Neil, a boutique hotel which opened in 2015. A 16-ton vault door which is swung open, contains a coffee maker and free bottles of Mother Earth beer inside a retro refrigerator. The limestone building with big ornate pillars out front and an analog clock on the corner, sets the tone for this exciting new hotel. The building was the home to the first registered elevator in North Carolina. A second-floor room with bright red walls and Chinese flair includes bunk beds in a small vault. The owner maintains his private quarters on the top floor.

Schmidt Artist Lofts in St. Paul Minnesota has been created from the Schmidt Brewery.

There are hundreds of adaptive reuse projects actively being renovated around the country. Many more than we have time to explore here but, I hope that you will consider the importance of the preservation work that is being done in both small towns and larger cities. Visit house museums, take walks through restored downtowns, immerse yourself in the past - both recent and ancient. Maybe you will even think about purchasing an old house or commercial space and putting it into service again, so it can continue to contribute to the built environment. The possibilities are endless.

The definition of adaptive reuse according to MIT is "to prolong the period from cradle-to-grave for a building by retaining all or most of the structural system, and as much a possible of other elements, such as cladding, glass and interior partitions."

Building Revivals on Granby Street, Norfolk, VA

Living History Exhibits Provide Glimpses of the Past

Christina Campbell Tavern, Williamsburg, VA

It is highly desirable that some exceptional buildings be preserved intact, without restoration, as surviving documents of a period or region. Simply protecting them from deterioration may sometimes prove to be the bests solution.   Charles Ravensway 1967 Chairman of "Planning for Preservation" seminar held in Williamsburg

The National Trust for Historic Preservation in the United States defines heritage tourism as «traveling to experience the places, artifacts and activities that authentically represent the stories and people of the past», and «heritage tourism can include cultural, historic and natural resources".

According to Cheryl Hargrove, the first director of Heritage Tourism for the National Trust and author of Cultural Heritage Tourism: Five Steps for Success and Sustainability, it is the fastest growing sector of tourism. It focuses on the unique combination of authentic experiences that define a particular place, person or event. Today's tourist is seeking a meaningful experience rather than just entertainment.

Heritage Areas, ranging from a single restored historic house museum in a small southern town to the larger exhibits like Colonial Williamsburg, Virginia, are valuable economic contributors to the providing regions in which they operate. The partnerships they create and facilitate, the efforts put forth to attract visitors, create economic development and preserve the culture, history, and assets of their regions truly make a difference to often depressed local communities.

These living history exhibits throughout our country offer us unique glimpses into the lifestyles and architecture of the past and inure us with a sense of time and place. They act as learning laboratories for us to participate in the everyday lives of our ancestors. They provide the preservationist an opportunity to familiarize themselves with regional building techniques and characteristics - techniques that were influenced by the existing lifestyle of those who built the environment. For instance, those who settled in the Northeast held more Puritanical and stricter religious beliefs so the homes tended to be more austere in appearance. While in the South more forgiving climes and freer religious rituals are reflected in less severe and more open architecture.

Other sites are more event specific like the Alamo, Gettysburg, Yorktown and Appomattox, VA battlefields. Each of these places commemorates the military action that took place there.

In Fredericksburg, VA a visit to Chatham Manor on the east side of the river, affords the visitor a very different perspective of how one thriving family farm was commandeered and became the staging ground for the Battle of Fredericksburg.

Colonial Williamsburg, VA, Sturbridge village in Massachusetts, Saint Augustine, Florida, Old Salem, North Carolina, Drayton Hall in Charleston South Carolina, are just a few of the more recognizable facilities that are available to experience. Visitors can expand and enhance their knowledge of the past by experiencing the variances between architectural styles and construction materials of the different periods. For example, the replication and restoration of structures in Colonial Williamsburg in the English style and the stabilization and original materials as existing at Drayton Hall. Other examples can be found in the Spanish influences in St. Augustine Florida, the Moravian in Old Salem, NC and the antebellum style in Charleston, SC. Diverse cultural differences are also apparent as depicted in the interpretive programming available at these sites.

Get out there and explore these exciting areas and get to know our history in a way that is also fun for you and your family!

Frontier Culture Museum, Staunton, VA

Appendices

Basic Preservation Terminology

Secretary of the Interiors' Standards of Rehabilitation

Historic Preservation Organizations

Resources for Greening Your Project

Sample Periodic Maintenance Checklist

Further Reading

Resources for Finding Older Homes

Stanley Hotel, Estes Park, Colorado Exterior Corbels

Basic Preservation Terminology

A unique Preservation language has evolved over the years. Let's take a look at some of the basic terms you should be familiar with when working on a project. It is vital that you are able to accurately communicate with craftspeople to avoid any misunderstandings of your desires.

<u>Adobe</u> - A kind of clay used as a building material, typically in the form of sun-dried bricks. Most often used in Spanish style architecture.

<u>American Bond Brick Pattern</u> - Also known as Common Bond. Courses of headers alternating with five or six courses of running bond stretchers. Also, can be used with Flemish bond alternating with courses of headers.

<u>Ashlar</u> - Squared stone blocks used in building.

<u>Balloon Framing</u> - A wooden building frame composed of machine-sawed scantlings fastened with nails, having studs rising the full height of the frame from first floor to roof.

Baluster/Balustrade - A baluster is one of a series of short vertical posts, often ornamental, used to support a rail. A railing composed of balusters and a top rail running along the edge of a porch, balcony, roof, or stoop is a balustrade.

Bargeboard (Vergeboard)

A board, often ornately carved, attached along the projecting edge of a pitched roof in front of a gable, where the roof extends over the wall, either covering the rafter that would otherwise be visible, or occupying its place. Also called a Vergeboard.

Batten - A narrow strip of wood used to cover the joints of wide boards in Board and Batten style siding and paneling which produces a geometric layered effect. Also called Barn Board since many barns and outdoor structures use this inexpensive siding method.

Capital - The upper most part of a classical column or other support. See Column Orders.

Cantilever - A projecting overhang, upper floor or beam that is supported only at one end.

Casement Window - A style of window that has sash that pivot outward on a vertical hinge at the jamb.

Caulking - A flexible material which is used to weather proof and seal the joins between two surfaces.

Coffered Ceilings -

A pattern of indentations or recesses in an overhead surface that is created by applying beams to the ceiling surface in a grid pattern. In architecture, a "coffer" is a sunken panel in a ceiling, including the interior surfaces of domes and vaults. Coffered ceilings have the effect of breaking up an interior space and making it feel more intimate and personal. However, tray ceilings offer a much more grandiose architectural style, making rooms feel larger, more open and totalitarian in how they are used. A less well-known method of creating coffers is offered by none other than Michelangelo. The Renaissance master manipulated the illusion of space with trompe l'oeil, a painting technique that tricks the eye into believing a certain reality. Michelangelo used his artistic skills to paint many of the three-dimensional moldings and crossbeams, creating the illusion of coffers in the most famous ceiling of all time, the Sistine Chapel in Vatican City, Rome.

<u>Colonnade</u> - A series of columns which support an entablature.

<u>Column Orders</u> - There are three recognized classical styles or orders of columns from ancient Greek and Roman architecture.

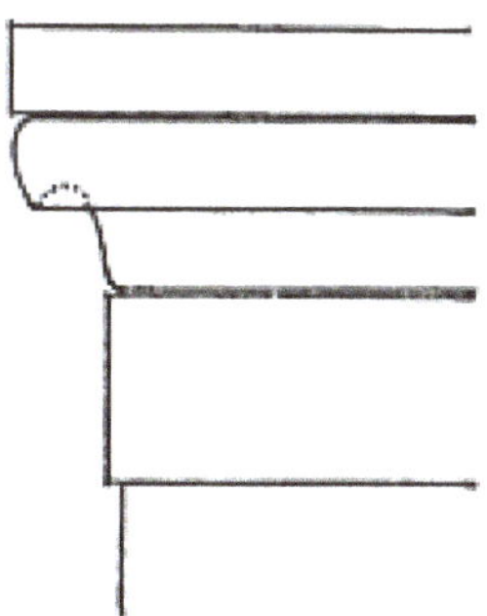

Doric is the earliest and simplest form with an unadorned capital and base. It can be fluted or smooth-surfaced. It originated in the western Doric region of Greece.

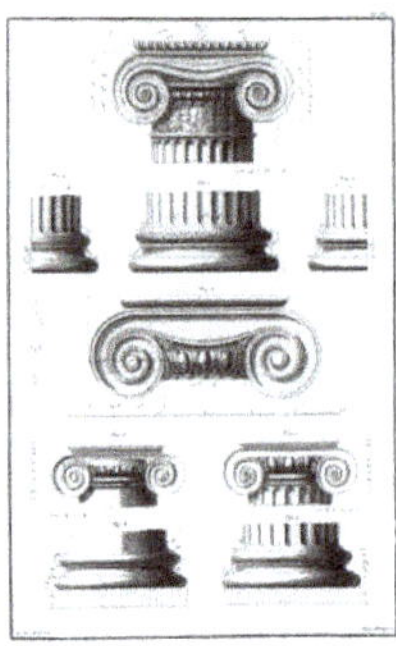

Ionic is always more slender than the Doric and is usually fluted The major features of the Ionic order are the volutes of its capital. This style was often used in Antebellum colonnades of late American Greek Revival plantation houses.

Corinthian This most ornate of the three orders is similar to the Ionic column, though it is more slender, and stands apart by its distinctive carved capital with Acanthus leaves.

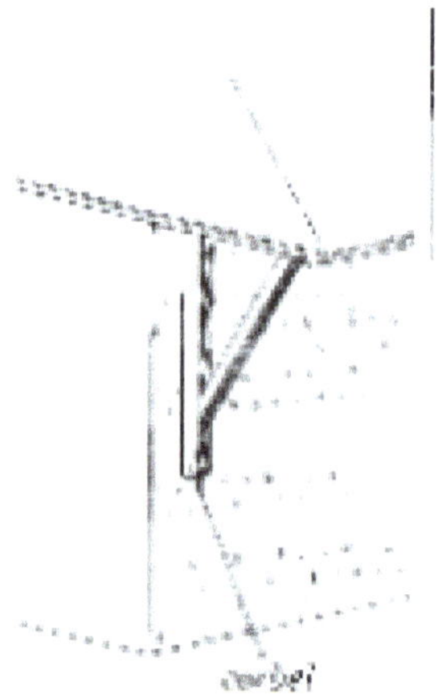

<u>Corbels</u> - Most simply put, this refers to a projecting arch or bracket which is sometimes molded or carved that acts as a system of support for a wall or floor. Corbels are built into walls to a depth that allows the pressure on the embedded portion to counteract the load on the exposed portion. The key difference between corbels and brackets is their width; corbels are generally thicker than brackets. They can also be very simple and

unadorned, as in the sketch. Both corbels and brackets are pieces that protrude from a wall and are designed to support some sort of weight. The key difference between corbels and brackets is their width; corbels are generally thicker than brackets.

<u>Crown Moldings</u> - Wood or plaster trim that runs between the top of an internal wall and a ceiling. The molding can vary from a single piece of molding or a complex pattern of many pieces to complement the style of the room.

Cupola - A cupola is a relatively small, most often dome-like, tall structure on top of a building. Often used to provide a lookout or to admit light and air, it usually crowns a larger roof. The name is a derivative of the Latin word cupula, which itself is a derivative of the Greek word kupellon, both meaning "small cup".

<u>Dentil</u> - One of a row of small rectangular toothlike blocks which form a molding below a cornice.

85

Dado (Wainscoting) - The lower paneling of an interior wall when it is specially deco-rated or faced with moldings. It is often made of oak.

Dormers, Bays, Turrets & Oriels - These types of windows - dormers, bays, turrets and oriels -share the common feature of windows that project from the house - in the roof or on the wall - and provide the pleasures of light and ventilation. A historical look at how windows expand into architectural appendages:

Dormers are placed within the roof line of the house allowing for more space inside what would otherwise be an attic space.

Bays project from the wall surface and allow for more space within a room as well.

In architecture, a turret is a small tower that projects vertically from the wall of a building such as those seen on Queen Anne architecture, most often on corners of the house itself.

Oriel Windows are a form of bay that does not reach the ground. Supported by corbels, brackets, or similar cantilevers, it is most commonly found projecting from an upper floor but is also sometimes used on the ground floor.

Double Hung Window - A style of window which had two sashes that are hung so that they pass each other vertically. They are described most often by the number of panes in each sash: six over six or nine over nine for example.

Eaves - The section of roof that overhangs exterior walls to protect from water entering the wall space.

English Bond - This other Common brick bond used in Colonial Virginia was used in structures dating from the 17th century until the late 18th century. It was replaced by common or American bond. The bond consists of alternating courses of headers and stretchers and was less ornamental than Flemish bond, but was very strong. Often used in foundations below Flemish wall surfaces.

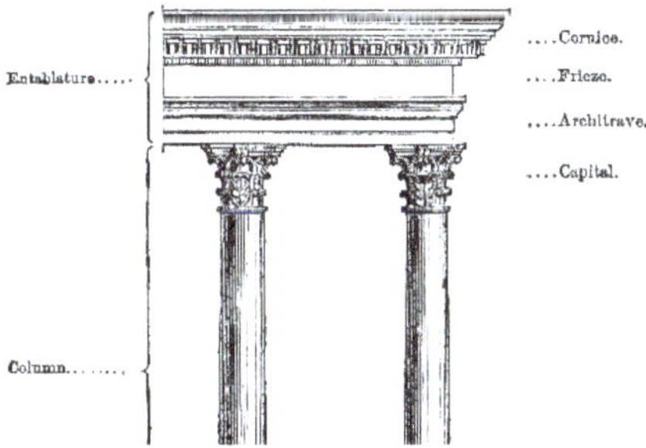

Entablature - The long flat structure above a classical column style comprised of the architrave, frieze and cornice.

Eyebrow Window - A small arched window that projects into the roof to allow light into an upper story.

Façade - This is the front or face of the building. In preservation, there are "Façade Grants" for the express purpose of restoring the facades of derelict buildings within a commercial district.

Fanlight - A fixed window sash over a door or another window which is usually curvi-linear in shape and has glazing bars or tracery set in radiating form resembling an open fan. It is also known as a lunette window. It can also be hinged as a transom.

Fenestration - The arrangement/placement of windows and doors on the elevations of a building.

Finial - A decorative ornament used on buildings and furniture

Flashing - A waterproof material most often metal which seals joins on roof openings and around chimneys.

Flemish Bond Brick Pattern - A brick wall pattern with alternating courses of head-ers (brick laid length wise) and stretchers (brick laid with ends showing). Used in the Chesapeake region in early 17th century and common in US until mid-19th century. Also known as block bond.

Foundation - The structure that the building rests on whether it is brick piers, a solid brick or stone wall or poured concrete.

Gable Roof - A single pitched roof that has end walls that are pointed at the top. Most often made of wood but can be brick.

88

Gambrel Roof (Mansard) - A type of roof popular on Dutch Colonial and Second Empire style homes. It is characterized by a pair of shallow pitched slopes above a steeply pitched slope on each side of a center ridge._

Half-Timbering - The type of wall treatment seen in Tudor architecture in which the spaces between heavy timbers are filled with brick stone or plaster sometimes called "nogging".

Hipped Roof - A roof style having slopes on all four sides,

HVAC - A term used commonly for heating, ventilating and air conditioning. The mechanical systems that control the temperature, air flow, humidity and airborne dust levels in a building.

Infill - A preservation term used to indicate the replacement of an existing building that cannot be saved with a new stylistically comparable structure.

Jamb - The material which forms the side of a door or window opening.

Joist - The series of timbers which form the framing for the floor.

Lath - The narrow strips of wood or metal that form the backing to support a plaster wall.

Light - The individual pane of glass in a window or door.

Lintel - A beam at the top of a door or window that is supported by upright members.

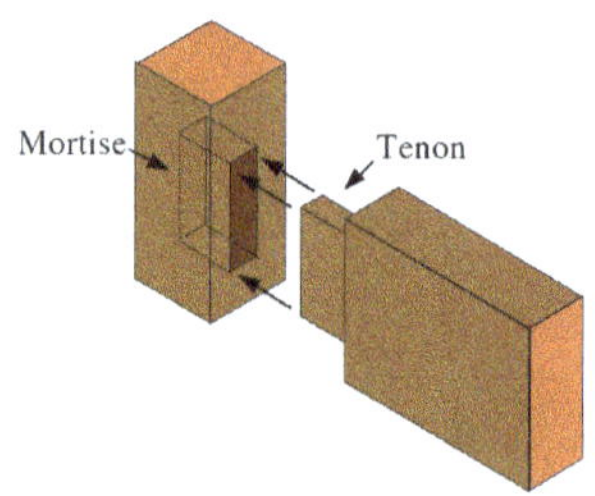

Mortise and tenon - A type of joinery which has a tongue (tenon) which fits into a recess (mortise).

Muntins/Mullions - The small moldings that separate panes of glass within a multi-paned window or door frame.

Palladian Style - Named for famed architect Andrea Palladio this tyle reflects classism, symmetry, and order. Windows feature arched topped center sections flanked by flat-topped sections.

<u>Pediment</u> - A triangular element at the top of a door, window or building.

<u>Pergola</u> - An outdoor garden feature forming a shaded walkway, passageway, or sitting area of vertical posts or pillars that usually support cross-beams and a sturdy open lattice, often upon which woody vines are trained.

<u>Pilaster</u> - An architectural element in classical architecture used to give the appearance of a supporting column, and to articulate an extent of wall, with only an ornamental function.

<u>Plasterboard</u> - Plasterboard or drywall or sheet rock was developed in the early 20th century as an economical and simpler replacement for plaster walls.

<u>Platform Framing</u> - A type of framing that has studs that that are single story and rest on the floors.

<u>Portico</u> - A pedimented porch supported by columns.

<u>Post and beam</u> - This type of construction was the predecessor of balloon framing. Post and beam construction uses large structural members to resolve loads; horizontal beams carry the load to vertical posts. The post and beam construction system creates large openings in between the posts.

<u>Quoins</u> - These are rectangular masonry blocks at the outside corner of a wall laid in a toothed pattern. They were used extensively in Renaissance style architecture. Stone quoins are used on stone or brick buildings. Brick quoins may appear on brick buildings, extending from the facing brickwork in such a way as to give the appearance of generally uniformly cut ashlar blocks of stone larger than the bricks.

<u>Rafter</u> - A structural framing member that forms the shape of the roof that the roofing material is attached to.

<u>Sash</u> -The parts of windows which hold the panes of glass and open or close.

<u>Sheathing</u> - Boards or sheets of wood that cover the framing and upon which the roofing material siding or wall finish is mounted.

<u>Shiplap Siding</u> - A type of Drop Lap siding with a tight "flush joint" profile. It is similar to tongue and groove but with a single overlap - usually 1/2" in depth but can be more or less depending on the width of the board 6", 8", 10" or the shiplap profile selected. This

type of siding has become extremely popular for those who are fans of Chip and Joanna Gaines' TV show Fixer Upper.

<u>Sill</u> - A beam or timber at the top of the foundation upon which the building rests or the bottom framing of a window or door.

<u>Soffit</u> - The underside of eaves

<u>Stucco</u> - An exterior wall finish made of lime, sand and Portland cement. The finish can be textured and/or painted.

<u>Transom</u> - An operable piece of glass or wood installed over a door to provide ventilation.

<u>Vapor Barrier</u> - A solid sheet of wood that protects the interior of the building from moisture either in the walls or roof.

Veranda - A long porch, often two story that runs along the entire front of a building especially those in the south.

Water Table - A projecting row of masonry above the foundation, that directs water away from the foundation thus protecting it.

"Rehabilitation" is defined as "the process of returning a property to a state of utility, through repair or alteration, which makes possible an efficient contemporary use while preserving those portions and features of the property which are significant to its historic, architectural, and cultural values."

The Standards are to be applied to specific rehabilitation projects in a reasonable manner, taking into consideration economic and technical feasibility.

Introduction to the Standards

The Secretary of the Interior is responsible for establishing standards for all programs under Departmental authority and for advising Federal agencies on the preservation of historic properties listed in or eligible for listing in the National Register of Historic Places.

The Standards for Rehabilitation (codified in 36 CFR 67 for use in the Federal Historic Preservation Tax Incentives program) address the most prevalent treatment. "Rehabilitation" is defined as "the process of returning a property to a state of utility, through repair or alteration, which makes possible an efficient contemporary use while preserving those portions and features of the property which are significant to its historic, architectural, and cultural values."

Initially developed by the Secretary of the Interior to determine the appropriateness of proposed project work on registered properties within the Historic Preservation Fund grant-in-aid program, the Standards for Rehabilitation have been widely used over the years--particularly to determine if a rehabilitation qualifies as a Certified Rehabilitation for Federal tax purposes. In addition, the Standards have guided Federal agencies in carrying out their historic preservation responsibilities for properties in Federal ownership or control; and State and local officials in reviewing both Federal and nonfederal rehabilitation proposals. They have also been adopted by historic district and planning commissions across the country.

The intent of the Standards is to assist the long-term preservation of a property's significance through the preservation of historic materials and features. The Standards pertain to historic buildings of all materials, construction types, sizes, and occupancy and encompass the exterior and interior of the buildings. They also encompass related landscape features and the building's site and environment, as well as attached, adjacent, or related new construction. To be certified for Federal tax purposes, a rehabilitation project must be determined by the Secretary to be consistent with the historic character of the structure(s), and where applicable, the district in which it is located.

As stated in the definition, the treatment "rehabilitation" assumes that at least some repair or alteration of the historic building will be needed in order to provide for an efficient contemporary use; however, these repairs and alterations must not damage or destroy materials, features or finishes that are important in defining the building's historic character. For example, certain treatments--if improperly applied--may cause or accelerate physical deterioration of the historic building. This can include using improper repointing or exterior masonry cleaning techniques, or introducing insulation that damages historic fabric. In almost all of these situations, use of these materials and treatments will result in a project that does not meet the Standards. Similarly, exterior additions that duplicate the form, material, and detailing of the structure to the extent that they compromise the historic character of the structure will fail to meet the Standards.

The Secretary of the Interior's Standards for Rehabilitation

The Standards (Department of Interior regulations, 36 CFR 67) pertain to historic buildings of all materials, construction types, sizes, and occupancy and encompass the exterior and the interior, related landscape features and the building's site and environment as well as attached, adjacent, or related new construction. The Standards are to be applied to specific rehabilitation projects in a reasonable manner, taking into consideration economic and technical feasibility.

1. A property shall be used for its historic purpose or be placed in a new use that requires minimal change to the defining characteristics of the building and its site and environment.

2. The historic character of a property shall be retained and preserved. The removal of historic materials or alteration of features and spaces that characterize a property shall be avoided.

3. Each property shall be recognized as a physical record of its time, place, and use. Changes that create a false sense of historical development, such as adding conjectural features or architectural elements from other buildings, shall not be undertaken.

4. Most properties change over time; those changes that have acquired historic significance in their own right shall be retained and preserved.

5. Distinctive features, finishes, and construction techniques or examples of craftsmanship that characterize a property shall be preserved.

6. Deteriorated historic features shall be repaired rather than replaced. Where the severity of deterioration requires replacement of a distinctive feature, the new feature shall match the old in design, color, texture, and other visual qualities and, where possible, materials. Replacement of missing features shall be substantiated by documentary, physical, or pictorial evidence.
7. Chemical or physical treatments, such as sandblasting, that cause damage to historic materials shall not be used. The surface cleaning of structures, if appropriate, shall be undertaken using the gentlest means possible.

8. Significant archeological resources affected by a project shall be protected and preserved. If such resources must be disturbed, mitigation measures shall be undertaken.

9. New additions, exterior alterations, or related new construction shall not destroy historic materials that characterize the property. The new work shall be differentiated from the old and shall be compatible with the massing, size, scale, and architectural features to protect the historic integrity of the property and its environment.

10. New additions and adjacent or related new construction shall be undertaken in such a manner that if removed in the future, the essential form and integrity of the historic property and its environment would be unimpaired.

THIS PROPERTY
HAS BEEN PLACED ON THE
NATIONAL REGISTER
OF HISTORIC PLACES
BY THE UNITED STATES
DEPARTMENT OF THE INTERIOR

The National Trust for Historic Preservation - This non-profit organization is the prime information source for anything regarding historic preservation. They publish a list of guidelines that is free to the public. You can get your copy of The Standard of Rehabilitation either on line or in print form from their web site. If you should be interested in listing your historic property on the National Register of Historic Places, you will need to follow these guidelines to the letter. Before you begin any work on your property, you will need to conduct a thorough survey of every room, document in photos all areas of the property (interior and exterior) and the streetscape it is situated within. It will also be most helpful to create a notebook of notes and ideas, room measurements photos, and necessary changes or repairs. This notebook should become your bible to guide you as you work.   Both physical and social history exists for your home. If you plan to have it listed, then you will need to conduct research on both its social and physical histories. If you are more interested in factual history to aid you in restoration and saving money, you will want to concentrate more on the physical history. Social history will help you connect with former owners and occupants. The listing process is very involved but worth it for more than just your own information. Some tax credit programs require registration to qualify. The Trust defines an historic house as "Historic houses are usually designated as significant examples of the cultural or physical developments of that community, state, or the entire nation, either because of their architecture or association with an important historical figure or event. They might also be related by a common theme with other buildings, such as an architectural movement." Contact this organization at savingplaces.org.

Preservation North Carolina (PNC) To quote their web site, "Preservation North Carolina, founded in 1939, promotes and protects the buildings and landscapes of our state's diverse heritage. Through its award-winning Endangered Properties Program, Preservation NC acquires endangered historic properties and then finds purchasers willing and able to rehabilitate them. It has saved more than 800 endangered historic properties, generating an estimated $350 million in private investment. Many of the saved properties have truly been community landmarks. Buyers have put these properties into a multitude of new uses, adding millions of dollars to local tax rolls and creating numerous jobs. Several of the larger properties have been adapted into affordable housing. More than 4,000 acres of open space have been placed under PNC's protective covenants, perpetually restricting their development. PNC's Endangered Properties Program is widely regarded as the nation's most successful program of its kind."

"At Preservation North Carolina we rescue old houses. And factory mills, schools, churches, general stores, and even the occasional big pink puppy. We're fondly referred to as "the animal shelter for old houses," it's a fun nickname, but a responsibility we take to heart. Through our nationally recognized and award-winning Endangered Properties Program we've rescued over 800 old, interesting, historic, sometimes abandoned, but always important properties. There's a story behind each one and we are committed to telling it." For more information and listings of available properties contact them at presnc.org.

New Mexico

State Historic Preservation Offices – SHPO

State Historic Preservation Officers (SHPO) in each state play a critical role carrying out many responsibilities in historic preservation. Surveying, evaluating, and nominating significant historic buildings, sites, structures, districts and objects to the National Register is one such key activity. To help find out if a historic place meets the National Register criteria and how the nomination process works in your state, contact the appropriate SHPO for assistance. Offices are listed by state.

The early stages of what would become the State Historic Preservation Office/Officer, or SHPO, was created in 1966, as part of the National Historic Preservation Act, or NHPA, to aid in the recognition and preservation of state and local government's historic fabric. Prior to its establishment, preservation was looked at through a national lens. Back then, objects of local historical significance were often deemed undeserving of preservation and usually completely overlooked. Through the National Historic Preservation Act and its implementation of the State Historic Preservation Program, the importance of the State Historic Preservation Office has grown along with its obligations and responsibilities.

"The State Historic Preservation Office's main purpose is to survey, document and nominate historic properties for the National Register of Historic Places, as well as to support their rehabilitation. In addition to physical conservation, they promote historic preservation on a smaller scale by helping local communities educate the public regarding local preservation issues.

On a wider scale, the State Historic Preservation Office is responsible for building and implementing the statewide historic preservation plan. This plan includes strategies for educating the public on issues of preservation, building a broad statewide survey and inventory of historic properties, assisting local governments in developing their own preservation plan, and much more.

Another important role of the SHPO is to serve as an advisor for the Section 106 review process. Section 106 refers to the portion of the National Historic Preservation Act that requires Federal agencies to consider the effects of its actions on historic properties, and gives an opportunity for comment and opposition based on potential adverse consequences."

From an article by: AUTHOR JON VALALIK

Building Materials Reuse Association – buildreuse.org. "We believe that the present linear economic model that relies on the consumption of new products and materials is unsustainable.   We know that the practice of reuse inherently recognizes and prioritizes existing community value. Reinvesting the wealth embodied in existing materials back into the communities from which they originated has enormous economic, environmental, cultural, and social potential. We're imagining a world without waste - and with the support of our members, we're taking collective strides to make this vision a reality."

Environmental and Energy Study Institute, eesi.org. The Environmental and Energy Study Institute is an independent, bi-partisan 501 non-profit organization that aims to promote environmentally sustainable societies. Based out of Washington, DC, EESI seeks to be a catalyst moving society away from environmentally damaging fossil fuels and toward a clean energy future.
Green Home Guide, greenhomeguide.com, This guide is a part of the U.S. Green Building Council. A LEED home is the best-performing home on the block. LEED, or Leadership in Energy and Environmental Design, is the most widely used green building rating system in the world. LEED provides a framework to create healthy, highly efficient and cost-saving green buildings. Designed and built for performance, every LEED home is third-party-inspected, tested and verified. LEED homes are gentler on the environment and on your wallet, delivering lower utility bills and requiring less maintenance. Simply put, LEED certified homes are higher quality. LEED certification is available for both single family and multifamily buildings.

The Rectory, circa 1880
111 Spiers Road, Como, NC

Architectura Element	Inspection	Every six months April 1 and Oct.1 Action	Once every year Action
Roofing	Inspect for loose or broken shingles	Replace shingles as necessary	Reinspect/ repair/ replace
Chimneys	Inspect flashing and brick	Seal flashing as needed repair brick	Reinspect and assess
Wood siding	Check for peeling/ chipped paint.	Scrape/repaint caulk open seams as needed	Repaint all siding
Windows and doors	Check panes for chips/breaks Check glazing. Check finishes	Reglaze as needed. Caulk frames as needed. Repaint trim as needed	Repaint all window frames and doors
Foundation	Check foundation/ piers for any damage. Check lattice foundation trim for damage	Repair damage as needed. Repaint, replace any trim as needed	Replace interior foundation trim layer for winter
Decking and porch	Inspect finishes on deck & porch floor. Check porch screen and frames for damage	Re-stain as needed. Repair screening	Re-stain deck and porch floor
Landscaping	Inspect all flower beds and walks	Weed, mulch trim plant materials, refresh walks with paver base	Assess all flower beds/landscaping for new materials/ work

Further Reading

A Field Guide to American Houses (Revised), The Definitive Guide to Identifying and Understanding America's Domestic Architecture, Virginia & Lee McAlester,2015

Inspecting a House, A guide for Buyers, Owners and Renovators, Carson Dunlop & Associates, Third Edition, Dearborn Trade Publishing, 2004

Old House Dictionary, An Illustrated Guide to American Domestic Architecture 100-1940, Steven J. Phillips. The Preservation Press, NATIONAL Trust for Historic Preservation, 1994.

Caring For Our Old House, A Guide for Owner and Residents, Judith Kitchen, National Trust for Historic Preservation, 1991.

Dictionary of Building Preservation, Edited by Ward Bucher, A.I.A., Press, John Wiley & Sons, Inc, 1996.

House Histories, A Guide to Tracing the Genealogy of Your Home, Sally Light, Golden Hill Press, Fifth Printing, 1995.

*Mail Order Homes, Sears Homes and Other Kit House*s, Rebecca I Hunter, Shire Publications, 2012.

Houses By Mail, A guide to Houses from Sears, Roebuck and Company, Katherine Cole Stevenson and H. Ward Jandl, National Trust for Historic Preservation, 1986.

Sears Modern Homes 1913, Sears Roebuck and Company, Dover Publications, 2006.

Resources for Finding Old Houses

The internet is a tremendous resource these days for finding older homes to rehab. Some of my favorites that seem to be consistent in content are listed below.

Facebook --

Old House Life with Michelle Bowers
Old Houses Under $50,000
For the Love of Old Houses
Circa Houses